CW00539982

L - 1155

Acceptable words

MANCHESTER
1824
Manchester University Press

Acceptable words

Essays on the poetry of Geoffrey Hill

JEFFREY WAINWRIGHT

Manchester University Press
Manchester and New York

distributed exclusively in the USA by Palgrave

Published by Manchester University Press
Oxford Road, Manchester M13 9NR, UK
and Room 400, 175 Fifth Avenue, New York, NY 10010, USA
www.manchesteruniversitypress.co.uk

Distributed exclusively in the USA by
Palgrave, 175 Fifth Avenue, New York,
NY 10010, USA

Distributed exclusively in Canada by
UBC Press, University of British Columbia, 2029 West Mall,
Vancouver, BC, Canada V6T 1Z2

British Library Cataloguing-in-Publication Data
A catalogue record for this book is available from the British Library

Library of Congress Cataloging-in-Publication Data applied for

ISBN   0 7190 6754 5 *hardback*
EAN   978 0 7190 6754 9

First published 2005

14 13 12 11 10 09 08 07 06 05   10 9 8 7 6 5 4 3 2 1

Typeset in Galliard by
D R Bungay Associates, Burghfield, Berks

Printed in Great Britain
by Bell & Bain, Glasgow

The preacher sought to find out acceptable words: and that which was
written was upright, even words of truth.

Ecclesiastes 12.10 (*AV*)

Words are never stone
except in their appearance.

'On the Sophoclean Moment in English Poetry', *Without Title*

To
Jon Glover

Contents

Acknowledgements

Most of these essays have appeared over a number of years as Geoffrey Hill's succeeding volumes have been published. I have revised them for this book but have tried to do so in ways that retain their original character as essays responding to the work as it appeared. They attempt to cover almost all Hill's poetry, including the remarkable body of poetry and prose published since 1996, and some work yet to appear in book form. The richness of his work means of course that these studies are at best preliminary. They are offered in the hope of benefiting his present readers and being of use to the many studies that will surely follow in the years to come.

I am very grateful to the editors who initially commissioned these essays, especially, and sorrowfully, to the late Jon Silkin of *Stand*, and the late William Cookson of *Agenda*. Peter Robinson, Michael Schmidt and René Gallet are the other editors I should like to thank.

The initial publications were as follows: 'Geoffrey Hill's *King Log*', *Stand*, Vol. 10 No. 1, 1968. 'Geoffrey Hill's "Lachrimae"', *Agenda*, Vol. 13 No. 3, 1976. 'Geoffrey Hill's *Tenebrae*', *Agenda*, Vol. 17 No. 1, 1979. 'The Mystery of the Charity of Charles Péguy', *Geoffrey Hill: Essays on His Work*, ed. Peter Robinson, Open University Press, 1985. '"History as Poetry": Geoffrey Hill: "Churchill's Funeral" and "De Jure Belli Ac Pacis"', *Agenda*, Vol. 34 No. 2, 1996. 'Geoffrey Hill: *The Triumph of Love*', *PN Review*, Vol. 26 No. 5, May-June, 13–21, 2000. An earlier version of '"Beauty is difficult": *Speech! Speech!*' was given as a conference paper at the colloque, 'La Poésie de Geoffrey Hill et la modernité', Université de Caen, mai 16–17, 2003. The title essay 'Acceptable Words', and the essays on *The Orchards of Syon*, *Scenes from Comus* and the Afterword appear here for the first time.

There are many others whose help, conversation, and commentary on Hill's work and on my own ideas have been invaluable to me over many years. First among them is Geoffrey Hill who has allowed me from time to time to see work prior to publication. I record my debt to one of the first from whom I learned about Hill's work, Ken Smith, who died in 2003. This book is dedicated to my friend of many years Jon Glover who gave me my copy of *For the Unfallen*.

I have also learned from and thank John Barnard, Laurence Coupe, Sara D'Orazio, René Gallet, Heather Glen, Jeremy Hawthorn, Avril Horner, John Kerrigan, Jennifer Kilgore, Antony Rowland, Michael Schmidt, Alistair Stead, Peter Walker, John Whale. Of course all responsibility for any failings of these essays rests entirely with me.

I am also very grateful to Matthew Frost and Kate Fox at Manchester University Press and to my copy editor John Banks.

I am grateful to Penguin Books for their kind permission to reproduce from the UK editions of Geoffrey Hill's poetry: *Collected Poems* (1985), *Canaan* (1996), *The Triumph of Love* (1998), *Speech! Speech!* (2000), *The Orchards of Syon* (2002) and *Scenes from Comus* (2005). In the USA: excerpts from *New and Collected Poems 1952–1992* (1994), *Canaan* (1996) and *The Triumph of Love* (1998) were reprined by pe mission of Houghton Mifflin Company. Excerpts from *Speech! Speech!* (2000), *The Orchards of Syon* (2002) and *Style and Faith* (2003) by permission of Counterpoint Press, a member of the Perseus Books Group. All rights reserved.

I acknowledge André Deutsch for quotations from *The Lords of Limit* (1984) and Oxford University Press *The Enemy's Country* (1991). For permission to quote from T. S. Eliot *Four Quartets* (1959) I thank Faber & Faber. For quotations from John Dunn, 'Political Obligation' in *The History of Political Theory and other essays* (1996), Cambridge University Press.

Abbreviations

Cn	*Canaan* (1996)
CP	*Collected Poems* (Penguin edition, 1985)
EC	*The Enemy's Country: Words, Contexture, and Other Circumstances of Language* (1991)
LL	*The Lords of Limit: Essays on Literature and Ideas* (1984)
MH	*Mercian Hymns* (1971)
OED	*Oxford English Dictionary*
Péguy	*The Mystery of the Charity of Charles Péguy* (1983; references to *CP*)
RV	*Rhetorics of Value* (2000)
Scenes	*Scenes from Comus* (2005)
SF	*Style and Faith* (2003)
SpSp	*Speech! Speech!* (2000)
Syon	*The Orchards of Syon* (2002)
TL	*The Triumph of Love: A Poem* (1998)
WT	*Without Title* (2006)

1 'Acceptable words'

> dirt and clinker-rammel, stomped / by snurring drayhorses
> (*Speech! Speech!* 75)

The first wonder of poetry lies in the immediate effects of language. How words are drawn from the myriad, their particular sounds heard and then associated by rhythm, and sometimes their visual appearance, constitutes the primary pleasure and amazement of verse. However great the repayments of re-reading and research might be, the experience of sensing the extraordinary in this dimension of language persists. It is the quality which led Milton in his pamphlet *Of Education* to identify poetry as 'more simple sensuous and passionate' than logic and rhetoric, not to exalt it above the philosophical arts but to insist upon 'what religious, what glorious and magnificent use might be made of poetry, both in divine and human things'.[1] Geoffrey Hill has frequently drawn attention to Milton's formulation 'simple sensuous and passionate' to describe the distinctive character of poetry. The achievement of such effects might finally be seen as intuitive. Undeniably, for the reader, the drawing together from the uncountable range of possibilities of a number of words that simply present themselves as 'right' seems not only a beauty but a mystery beyond the laws of logic or rhetoric. In his essay 'Poetry as "Menace" and "Atonement"' (*The Lords of Limit*, 1984) Hill carefully discusses such experience from the point of view of composition and endorses Yeats's description that 'a poem comes right with a click like the closing of a box' (*LL* p. 2).

Hill's poetry abounds with lines that offer the kind of wonder I am trying to describe. The first and last lines of his first book, *For the Unfallen* (1959), present different tones but a similar kind of exact felicity. 'Genesis' begins

> Against the burly air I strode
> Crying the miracles of God.
> (*CP* p. 15)

At least two things arrest us here. The first is rhythmic as the regular stresses of the tetrameter fall confidently through the first line, mostly on strong consonants, 'Against the burly air I strode', and push on through the run-on continuation to the reversed, first syllable stress of line 2, 'Crying …' Then that line stretches out with just the central stress on 'miracles' before the closure upon 'God'. Thus the two lines bristle with an assertive, muscular energy which seems to be suddenly caught up in wonder in line 2 as the unstressed syllables and the softer consonant and lighter stress of 'miracles' makes the line float in comparison with the sturdy tread of the opening. The second feature is the oxymoron 'burly air'. As will appear in the succeeding essays, oxymoron was to be an important, and highly theorised, device for Hill. Here the heft of the strongly consonantal 'burly' contrasts with the sound of 'air' which is so light as to be hardly voiced. Yet the air, the wind, is thus given this sense of thick-set physical presence so that it and 'I' are shouldering each other like two wrestlers. These remarks concentrate only upon the sensuous qualities of the words. Another moment of consideration would have us note that 'burly' also carries the important, if now less familiar, connotation of 'stately' or 'noble', and that the unusual use of 'crying' as a transitive verb makes possible an ambiguity which becomes vital to the poem as a whole, that of the cry as announcement or summons as well as of emotion or pain.

The last poem in *For the Unfallen* is the satiric address 'To the (Supposed) Patron'. It closes:

> For the unfallen – the firstborn, or wise
> Councillor – prepared vistas extend
> As far as harvest; and idyllic death
> Where fish at dawn ignite the powdery lake.
>
> (*CP* p. 57)

In its poised, slow easefulness this last line has quite a different tone from the urgent opening of 'Genesis'. Its languor comes of the extended sounds of 'fish', 'dawn', 'powdery' and 'lake', and in the way that the extra syllable of 'powdery' stretches out the otherwise exactly measured iambic pentameter – the only truly regular one in a poem whose scepticism is held in a series of metrical switches and stops. We will wonder what 'ignite', an altogether more peremptory sound, is doing in the middle of this dreamy line, and in what sense the bubbles and ripples of fish rising to feed might be said to be 'igniting' the water? Thinking of this, a lake that is so peacefully still it lies dusted, perhaps with pollen, becomes '(gun)powdery', and there is some insidious shudder in this romanticised image of 'idyllic death'. Or it might be that the line is so poised that 'ignites' works simply as hyperbole, an ingeniously unexpected effect. It is a memorable, and mysteriously beautiful line. It is also a studiously 'beautiful' line.

The import of what I am emphasising here as a prime achievement of Hill's poetry might seem to draw us towards the familiar parallel with music and the notion of 'pure poetry', that is a composition which strikes our passions through its immediate sensuous effects and therefore possesses an innocent simplicity. I do want to insist upon the power of such immediacy in Hill's verse, but even the most preliminary reading of lines like those above shows how brief the interval is before we are struck by the reverberations of meaning mobile within the sound and shape of individual words and their sequences. Here is another example, from 'Pisgah', published in *Canaan* (1996). The poem is a memory of the poet's father recalled in his garden:

> around you the cane loggias, tent-poles, trellises,
> the flitter of sweet peas caught in their strings[.]
>
> (*Cn* p. 52)

I want to concentrate here upon the second of these lines – 'the flitter of sweet peas caught in their strings' – and especially the choice of the word 'flitter' which most distinguishes the description. The more expected word here might have been 'flutter', which is very close in both in meaning and sound, or, to emphasise the sense of light, unstable, fleeting movement, the line might have been arranged to accommodate the verb 'flit'. But the noun 'flitter', crucially lighter in its voicing than 'flutter', carries an extra meaning which is that 'flitter' is a form of decoration, tiny squares of thin metal, often brightly coloured (*Oxford English Dictionary*). The frail, diaphanous, multi-coloured, endlessly moving petals of sweet peas are more precisely pictured through 'flitter' than any possible alternative. That they are 'caught' in the strings they grow along also gives a hint of imprisonment, as of trapped butterflies, and so the whole image contributes to the sense of the fragility, and the helpless dance of memory. 'Flitter' therefore achieves sensuous immediacy but also a rightness that depends upon the full possibilities of its meanings. It would not be surprising to know that Hill also intends the echo that the *OED* provides in one of its citations on 'flitter', Keats's line from *Lamia*: 'And but the flitter-wingèd verse must tell / For truth's sake what woe afterwards befel.' The box clicks shut with such a discovery as 'flitter', certainly as a result of the intuitive impulse that is part of poetic composition, but also by virtue of conscious thought and labour. It is the capacity of poetry to encompass both kinds of mental action within its forms that means that poetry is not an exchangeable form of discourse.

Plain speaking still an order I believe.
('To the Teller of Fortunes' *Without Title*)

In that line from *Lamia* Keats is turning dismissal of poetry against itself, anticipating and absorbing the derogation of poetry as slight and insubstantial in order to enter the gentle claim that it can act 'for truth's sake'. In the traditional antithesis 'flitter-wingèd verse' is opposed by down-to-earth 'plain speaking'. This might be seen as part of a very ancient war indeed. Its modern phase broke out in earnest with 'the advancement of learning' in the seventeenth century where the programmes of the new rationalism addressed what Thomas Sprat of the Royal Society called 'the cheat of words'. Respect for empirical truth, and the conviction that eloquence had served to obscure it, drove Sprat's demand for language to 'return back to primitive purity, and shortness, when men deliver'd so many things, almost in an equal number of words'. The philosopher Berkeley complained that since 'words are so apt to impose upon the understanding I am resolved in my inquiries to make as little use of them as I possibly can'. In this temper it is unsurprising to find poetry termed 'a kind of ingenious nonsense'.[2]

It is in part because Geoffrey Hill's work, in poetry and prose, is in perpetual struggle with 'plain speaking' that he is drawn to write so often on seventeenth-century subjects. In his essay 'The Tartar's Bow and the Bow of Ulysses' in *The Enemy's Country* (1991), he quotes Thomas Hobbes: 'there is scarce any word that is not made *equivocal* by divers contextures of speech, or by diversity of pronunciation and gesture'. Because Hobbes inveighed so sharply against the 'Abuses' of speech which he saw as corresponding to its 'Uses' – including the use of words metaphorically, 'that is, in other sense than that they are ordained for; and thereby deceive others'[3] – he is often counted among the programmatic purists with regard to language. Hill dissents from this view. In 'The Tartar's Bow ...' he continues:

> It will be objected that Hobbes, like Bacon, regarded equivocation, all forms of ambiguity in language, as 'intolerable' and worked for their eradication; and, from that, it may be concluded that he and Bacon were at liberty to stand aloof from 'the intolerable wrestle | With words and meanings'. Empirical observation confirms that this is not so. Bacon, in *The Advancement of Learning*, argues that 'wordes, as a *Tartars* Bowe, doe shoote backe vppon the vunderstanding of the wisest, and mightily entangle, and peruert the Iudgement.' He is not offering an aloof analysis for, as he says, 'it is not possible to diuorce our selues from these fallacies and false

appearances, because they are inseparable from our Nature and Condition of life'. (*EC* pp. 22–3)

This is essentially Hill's position: that the ambition for transparency, simplicity, 'purity' as envisaged by a Thomas Sprat is impossible. It is the 'plain speakers' for all their professed commitment to practicality and the down-to-earth who are in fact otiose, for 'our Nature and Condition of life' requires that we live in 'the *negotium* of language of itself' (*EC* p. 10). In the above quotation Hill alludes to T. S. Eliot's *Four Quartets*, and Eliot's lines from 'Burnt Norton' share Hobbes's and Bacon's experience of language:

> Words strain,
> Crack and sometimes break, under the burden,
> Under the tension, slip, slide, perish,
> Decay with imprecision, will not stay in place,
> Will not stay still.[4]

Hill has found resignation in the later Eliot's lamenting of language. In 'Poetry as "Menace" and "Atonement"' he takes him to task for a remark in his essay 'Poetry and Drama':

> Eliot speaks of 'a fringe of indefinite extent, of feeling which we can only detect, so to speak, out of the corner of the eye and can never completely focus ... At such moments, we touch the border of those feelings which only music can express'. As Eliot well knew, however, a poet must also turn back, with whatever weariness, disgust, love barely distinguishable from hate, to confront 'the indefinite extent' of language itself and seek his 'focus' there. In certain contexts the expansive, outward gesture towards the condition of music is a helpless gesture of surrender, oddly analogous to that stylish aesthetic of despair, that desire for the ultimate integrity of silence, to which so much eloquence has been so frequently and indefatigably devoted. (*LL* p. 9)

Words will have meanings, and if life is made difficult because, as Hobbes writes, words, 'besides the signification of what we imagine of their nature, have a signification also of the nature, disposition, and interest of the speaker' so that 'one man calleth *Wisdome*, what another calleth *feare*; and one *cruelty* another *justice*', this is part of the negotiation we must make however 'intolerable'. For Hill this negotiation has produced a poetry continually marked by deep suspicion of the art itself, perpetually aware of its artifice and of the dangers of a self-satisfied confidence in authenticity: 'demanding to be loved, demanding love in the form of recognition and "absolution"' (*LL* p. 17). Often, especially in later work such as *Speech! Speech!* (2000), this has resulted in a deliberate brutalisation of poetry which, so far from 'demanding to be loved', defies acceptance: 'Incantation or incontinence – the lyric cry?' (*TL* p. 79). For Hill there is escape from the wrestle neither in the direction of seeking only the immediate character of language, the 'music' of 'pure poetry', nor in a manner which thinks to disarm 'the cheat of words' by the complaisance of 'plain speaking'.

That all this is far from an arcane concern can be seen when the sensuous immediacy of verbal effect is combined with popularising plainness. In his *Paris Review* interview of 2000 Hill claims 'that tyranny requires simplification' and adduces the German scholar Theodore Haecker who

> argues, with specific reference to the Nazis, that one of the things the tyrant most cunningly engineers is the gross over-simplification of language, because propaganda requires that the minds of the collective respond primitively to slogans of incitement. And any complexity of language, any ambiguity, any ambivalence implies intelligence. Maybe an intelligence under threat, maybe an intelligence that is afraid of the consequences, but nonetheless an intelligence working in qualifications and revelations ... resisting, therefore, tyrannical over-simplification.[5]

One of the most insistent of Hill's themes is that words are never for the wind. To speak, to write, is to act. This is the other reason for his preoccupation with the writing of the sixteenth and seventeenth centuries where for Wyatt, Surrey, Tyndale, Donne, Taylor, Milton, Hobbes, Dryden 'words, contexture, and other circumstances of language' could be a matter of exile, imprisonment or death. The same is true of his regard for 'the endurance of poets' such as Campanella, Desnos, Hernandez and Mandelstam, and for the German resistance to Hitler, Bonhoeffer, von Haeften and von Moltke, and for Okigbo, Nzeogwu and Fajuyi who died in the Nigerian–Biafran war.

The nature of 'speech acts' which, and in which circumstances, can be said to be 'performative', that is commit the speaker to a specific action, is the subject of Hill's painstaking discussion of the philosopher J. L. Austin in the essay 'Our Word Is Our Bond' (*LL* pp. 138-59). I discuss this in a later essay in connection with *The Mystery of the Charity of Charles Péguy*, but it includes Hill's rigorous discussion of Austin's contention that words uttered in a poem 'would not be seriously meant'.

It might easily be said that the context in which a poem is written is all, and therefore question Hill's claim that his utterances might be taken as seriously as 'acts' when compared with those mentioned above. Indeed it could be said – to invoke his own comparison – that, so far from being able to own the gravity of a Nadezhda Mandelstam, the words of a modern English poet are a less 'performative' than those of a knitting editor who can plausibly claim 'if I make a mistake there are jerseys all over England with one arm longer than the other' (*LL* p. 7). What is the justice of the ethical demand Hill puts upon his work?

Night and fog it is then, comrades (*SpSp* 88)

In the seventh section of *The Mystery of the Charity of Charles Péguy* Hill quotes his protagonist: 'Péguy said / "why do I write of war? | Simply because / I have not been there"' (*CP* p. 192). There is a voice in *The Triumph of Love* which sees the prominence of the two world wars, the Shoah, and other extremities in Hill's poetry as 'obsession': 'This is quite dreadful – he's become obsessed. / There you go, there you go – narrow it down to *obsession*!' (*TL* p. 21). Hill's severe reflexiveness towards his own voices has been there from the beginning: 'The dead are my obsession this week / / But may be lifted away', he wrote in *For the Unfallen* (*CP* p. 49). 'Obsession' is a narrowing down because it is morally empty. I shall try to show that Hill's wariness of obsession is part of his concentration upon these events and that Péguy's phrase 'Simply because I have not been there' is at the heart of his witness.

The matter begins with Geoffrey Hill's precise historical situation. Born in 1932 in the English West Midlands, his boyhood was inevitably dominated by the fears and excitements of the Second World War: 'I loved the battle anthems and the | gregarious news', he recalls in *Mercian Hymns* XXII (*CP* p. 126). Growing into maturity in the years after the war with the mounting awareness of the Shoah, of the atom bombs on Japan and of local sacrifice and bereavement, the sense of being a war survivor mounts, and an awed fascination with 'the varied dead' haunts *For the Unfallen*. The first duty is witness, attention, as the variation on Laurence Binyon's title indicates. Then there is a dwelling on the archaeological layers of 'the speechless dead', as for instance from the Battle of Towton in 'Funeral Music', and the consequent questions about civilisation such as Ezra Pound had posed in the aftermath of the First World War in 'Hugh Selwyn Mauberley': 'There died a myriad ... for two gross of broken statues, / For a few thousand battered books.'[6] Pound's conjunction of 'a botched civilisation' and art is similar to Walter Benjamin's uncompromising sentence

in his 'Theses on the Philosophy of History': 'There is no document of civ-
ilization which is not at the same time a document of barbarism.'[7] Hill's
reflexiveness always carries the weight of these challenges to art: he makes
'an elegy for myself' and his exact contemporary commemorated in
'September Song' – '*born 19.6.32 – deported 24.9.42*' – has no life at all (*CP*
p. 67). In *Canaan* and *Speech! Speech!* he remembers the Nigerian poet
Christopher Okigbo, 1932–1967. The persistent question is what does
the moral luck of living this life, not theirs, mean for him, for his readers
and our polity? This is not narrow obsession but a complex deliberation of
our society's greatest ethical demand.

> Shocks, alignments, brake-fluids, slackened / memory, checked
> and adjusted. (*SpSp* 45)

Certainly Hill feels this demand personally but it is also a matter for the
polity at large, and his work is dominated by visions of the public realm.
Mercian Hymns (1971; *CP* pp. 105–34) is a conjuncture of autobiogra-
phy and the public inheritance. What is remembered therefore is personal
and national: the luminous details of a particular childhood and what 'he
left behind coins, for his lodging, and traces of | of red mud' (*MH* XXX).
'He', King Offa, is master of Mercia, 'overlord of the M5' (I), but also
a European figure of substance. He is a primitive tyrant and a modern
man who established laws and a sound coinage, the necessary elements
of good governance. He is anticipated too, I think, in 'To the (Supposed)
Patron' where the rhythms and modes of description resemble those of
Mercian Hymns:

> Prodigal of loves and barbecues,
> Expert in the strangest faunas, at home
> He considers the lilies, the rewards.
> There is no substitute for a rich man.
> (*CP* p. 57)

Both repellent and fascinating, to some extent the boy identifies with his
strangeness:

> 'A boy at odds in the house, lonely among brothers.'
> But I, who had none, fostered a strangeness; gave
> myself to unattainable toys.
> (VI)

His authority too appeals to the child's dreams of power, instanced in
particular in the beating of 'Ceolred' for losing his toy aeroplane.

Afterwards, 'leaving Ceolred, he journeyed for hours, | calm and alone, in his private derelict sandlorry | named *Albion*' (VII). Comic as this episode is, it carries a strange, even fearsome, loneliness. Deeply attached to the intimate rub of family, school, church and locality, especially in wartime, the boy is nevertheless estranged:

> Dreamy, smug-faced,
> sick on outings – I who was taken to be a king of
> some kind, a prodigy, a maimed one.
>
> (V)

When the time comes to leave he is exchanging a world of warm, kitcheny routines for something remotely other:

> So, murmurous, he withdrew from them. Gran lit the
> gas, his dice whirred in the ludo-cup, he entered
> into the last dream of Offa the King.
>
> (XXIX)

But vying with the glamour of Offa's power and charisma is the consciousness of his tyranny. The coins may be 'handsome as Nero's' and the 'exactness of design was to deter imitation' but

> muti-
> lation if that failed. Exemplary metal, ripe for
> commerce. Value from a sparse people, scrapers of
> salt-pans and byres.
>
> (XI)

Offa's power, wealth and success is extracted from the common people. He does impose order, but the source and arbitrariness of his power must question its legitimacy. Here we can recognise a major theme in political philosophy. Legitimacy is the cornerstone of all governance, but how is it derived, and what therefore is the source of political obligation? On what basis and understanding do we grant power to authority?

For the first edition of *King Log* Hill used as epigraph a phrase from Bacon's *The Advancement of Learning*: 'From moral virtue let us pass on to matter of power and commandment ...' For Hill pondering the relationship between 'moral virtue' and 'power and commandment' is central to his work. The implication of Bacon's phrase as Hill fades it away is that 'virtue' and 'power' do not co-exist: to consider one we must pass *from* the other. Again the seventeenth century is an important site of discussion. As England eventually deposed the idea – and for eleven years the person – that authority resides in a monarch legitimised by God, so

a new basis for political legitimacy had to be found. Essentially, for
Hobbes and John Locke, this new legitimacy derived from pragmatic,
enlightened self-interest. Hobbes famously described life in 'the state of
nature' as 'nasty, brutish and short', and so to mitigate the insecurity of
what would otherwise be a 'war of all against all' a powerful central
authority, Leviathan, is necessary. The polity is defined by a form of con-
tract in which the people (narrowly defined then as male and property-
owning) surrender a measure of independence of action in return for
security: Offa's laws and coins.

In the first of his Tanner Lectures on the nature of intrinsic value,
Rhetorics of Value (2000), Hill states that

> *Leviathan*, whatever else it is or is not, is a tragic elegy on the extinc-
> tion of intrinsic value ... Hobbes's despair, in *Leviathan*, arises from
> the extinction of personal identity, which he in turn identifies with
> intrinsic value in the person of the young Royalist Sidney
> Godolphin, killed in the Civil War. [8]

John Dunn in his nuanced and superbly instructive essay 'Political
Obligation' describes Hobbes as having 'attempted to derive compre-
hensive political obligation from nothing but expediency and rational-
ity'.[9] Hitherto Dunn has delivered a careful exposition of the undoubted
power of Hobbes's theory of political legitimacy, but his next sentence
is: 'But his attempt did not succeed.' For the reasons Dunn thinks this is
so I refer readers to his essay, though I shall continue to make use of his
ideas in endeavouring to explain why Hobbes's attempt does not suc-
ceed for Hill.

Hill's proposal that *Leviathan* is 'a tragic elegy on the extinction of
intrinsic value' must come from recognising that Hobbes's theory results
from the conviction that nothing is to be expected from the exercise of
'moral virtue' in governance. His theory of obligation is essentially
defensive, 'prudent' in Dunn's phraseology (p. 82). It follows, writes
Dunn, upon

> its sharp focus upon human vulnerability and on those human qual-
> ities which most endanger the vulnerable in practice. The justifica-
> tion of state power, if it is to rest anywhere stable at all, must depend
> finally upon the peculiar urgency for every human being of meet-
> ing this particular need: on a mutual relation between protection
> and obedience. (p. 69)

One pragmatic reason why Hobbes's theory does not wholly 'succeed'
must be the unlikelihood that this 'mutual relation' will always be in

balance. But Hill's objection must include reasons of a different kind. It is, I think, that this vision of contracting parties extinguishes 'personal identity', 'the intrinsic value of the person', as anything other than the being calculating the equation of present and future protection and obedience. If *Leviathan* is indeed a 'tragic elegy' mourning Godolphin then it must be because his new theory has no *use* for the man he loved and admired. Except that the particulars of identity cannot be so extinguished. Dunn identifies Hobbes's theory as utilitarian and 'necessarily directed towards the future, the sole setting which we have the power to affect by our actions' (p. 82). But agents exercising this power have histories that are both personal and social, and utilitarianism, as Dunn says, is constantly frustrated by the influence these have on decisions people make. Powerfully, Dunn writes: 'no human agent can apprehend the cumulative outcome of human history or know how all human beings now are' (p. 84). From such an acknowledgement we can see how Geoffrey Hill's insistence in his work upon the importance of history and memory both recognises reality and understands the nature of personal identity. The boy who withdraws to enter 'the last dream of Offa the King' cannot leave behind him the whirr of dice in the ludo cup or the car-park of the 'Stag's Head'.

> I
> wish greatly to believe: that Bromsgrove
> was, and is, Goldengrove; that the Orchards
> of Syon stand as I once glimpsed them.
> But there we are: the heartland remains
> heartless – that's the strange beauty of it.
>
> (*Syon*, XXXVIII)

The loss and gain of remembrance is unfathomable, but in the late work Hill has come to fear its repression as all too possible: 'I am saying (simply) / what is to become of memory? Yes – I know – / I've asked that before' (*TL* CXXXVIII). Elsewhere in *The Triumph*, berating one of his caricature critics he writes of 'a daily acknowledgement / of what is owed the dead' (CXIX). Here we arrive at a very important concept for Hill. In 'Political Obligation' Dunn describes one alternative to the Hobbesian 'obligation of prudence' as 'an obligation of gratitude'. Dunn delineates the differences:

> Obligations of prudence are rational, modern and, at least incipiently, utilitarian. They are fixated upon the future. Obligations of gratitude, by contrast, are decidedly more traditional. They focus obsessively upon the past; and their rationality is today very actively in dispute. (p. 83)

Hill, I suggest, accepts his political obligation very much in terms of gratitude, most directly from family and the force of the war upon his upbringing and imagination:

> At home the curtains were drawn. The wireless boomed
>   its commands. I loved the battle-anthems and the
>   gregarious news.
>
> Then, in the earthy shelter, warmed by a blue-glassed
>   storm-lantern, I huddled with stories of dragon-
>   tailed airships and warriors who took wing im-
>   mortal as phantoms.
>
> (MH XXII)

Later this excited cosiness gives way to different knowledge of 'places where grief has stood mute– / howling for half a century' (*TL* LXXVII). 'Why do I write of war? Simply because / I have not been there.' Of course Hill can be accused of focusing 'obsessively on the past', and of nostalgia. But whether or not he or we might believe that 'the obligation of gratitude' could or should replace 'prudence' it is hard to decry it. As Dunn says in the process of his exhaustive balancing of arguments, 'Duties of gratitude and fairness may be conceptually well-shaped to restrain the hastiness and self-righteousness of an ultra-individualistic political culture' (p. 87). Such a culture must be forgetful as it hurries after modernisation, always replacing, always certain of itself, like British imperialism in India:

> Suppose they sweltered here three thousand years
> patient for our destruction. There is a greeting
> beyond the act. Destiny is the great thing,
> true lord of annexation and arrears.
> ('A Short History of British India II'; *CP* p. 156)

The masses whose toil made the modern world through industrialisation must also be subsumed by 'Destiny'. But Hill does not forget:

> It is one
> thing to celebrate the 'quick forge', another
> to cradle a face hare-lipped by the searing wire.
>
> Brooding on the eightieth letter of *Fors Clavigera*,
>   I speak this in memory of my grandmother, whose
>   childhood and prime womanhood were spent in the
>   nailer's darg.
>
> (MH XXV; CP p. 129)

Such a life is mocked by contemporary cupidity. 'To the High Court of Parliament *November 1994*':

> Where's the probity in this –
> > the slither-frisk
> to lordship of a kind
> as rats to a bird-table?
> > > (*Canaan* p. 1)

Remembrance, even speaking in memory and 'simple gratitude' involves human relations and human histories, including conscience – 'I am ashamed and grieve' begins that poem on his father, 'Pisgah'.

This world is different, belongs to them – (*Péguy* 4)

To read through Geoffrey Hill's work is to be aware of a great sense of alienation from 'this world', a sense that deepens in the later work. This might be understood as the persistence of the estrangement of the boy of *Mercian Hymns* into those bitter mental struggles of adulthood that are more and more openly professed in more recent work, including the rages and shames: '*Mea / culpa*, ma'am, a nervous tort' (*TL*, CIX). '*Mania*' is the published theme of the most recent collection, *Without Title* (forthcoming 2006), and in the beginning of this poem, 'In Ipsley Church Lane 1', we can see how the natural world is mediated through terrifying emotion:

> More than ever I see through painters' eyes.
> The white hedge-parsleys pall, the soot is on them.
> Clogged thorn-blossom sticks, like burnt cauliflower,
> to the festered hedge-rim. More than I care to think
> I am *as one* coarsened by feckless grief.
> Storm cloud and sun together bring out the yellow of stone.

The brilliant perception of the simile, 'like burnt cauliflower', with its comic twitch of domestic frustration enters a note of bathos which along with the familiar locution 'more than I care to think' first undermines and then intensifies the direct pain of 'I am *as one* coarsened by feckless grief.' More and more, as I hope my essays on the later work will show, the stresses of the poet's own – and owned – mental states become more prominent in the work. Hill's sense of Charles Péguy as a kindred spirit – eccentric, obdurate, at odds, like Pound's Mauberley perpetually 'out of key with his time', justified but only doubtfully so – seems more and more evident in the light of the work since. Here, at the outset of section 4 of

The Mystery of the Charity of Charles Péguy, is some of the portrait, and it includes two phrases close to those Hill uses as titles for his books of essays:

> This world is different, belongs to them –
> the lords of limit and of contumely.
> It matters little whether you go tamely
> or with rage and defiance to your doom.
>
> This is your enemies' country which they took
> in the small hours an age before you woke,
> went to the window, saw the mist-hewn
> statues of the lean kine emerge at dawn.
>
> (CP p. 186)

This sense of being beset by 'the lords of limit and of contumely', at bay in 'your enemies country' is recurrently present. At the beginning of 'Unhappy Circumstances', the first essay in *The Enemy's Country* (having already provided an extensive note on his title) Hill evokes Aubrey's portrait of Thomas Hobbes among 'the witts at Court', happy enough in repartee but 'reluctant to "conclude hastily" in questions of weight and import'. Then 'he turned and winded and compounded … as if he had been at Analyticall worke' (*EC* p. 1). Hill's complaint is that 'this world' is so wedded to the instant it will not tarry to hear conclusions that have been, of necessity, 'turned and winded and compounded'. This is the object of the satire of *Speech! Speech!* (2000) where the welter of media communication constitutes itself as 'the world' much as the seventeenth-century court did. But there are 'questions of weight and import' in the world where 'we vaunt and suffer' ('Funeral Music 8'; *CP* p. 77), and it would be shallow to attempt to comprehend Hill's fifty-plus years of work attending to them as neurosis.

When all else fails CORINTHIANS will be read / by a man in too-tight shoes. (*Speech! Speech!* 114)

> 'This world' might all be understood through religious faith:
>   Blackened as Rouault's *Miserere*, a body
>   splays for the camera, the camera
>   staying put, except it probes further
>   the human midden.
>
> (*Syon* XLIV)

As part of a depiction of the 1944 Battle of Normandy this image compounds a soldier's corpse with an image of the crucifixion and the voyeurism of the porno shot. This is the 'human midden', in Christian terms the fallen world. In the second of his *Rhetorics of Value* lectures, Hill declares himself 'attached ... to a form of belief in Original Sin, one that is probably not too far removed from the orthodox' (*RV* p. 271), but the nature of the poet's religious faith as it appears in his work has not always been so straightforwardly put. What has always been clear however is that Judaeo-Christianity has always held a great explanatory power for Hill, great, and perhaps sufficient: 'There is no bloodless myth will hold' ('Genesis', *CP* p. 16). Its whole discourse, words and images – often beautiful – is dyed into the culture he has inherited. Faith aside, working in language, and especially with poetic forms, means that 'From the depths of the self we rise to a concurrence with that which is not-self' ('Poetry as "Menace" and "Atonement"', *LL* p. 3), and for Hill the 'not-self' includes the Judaeo-Christian legacy. It offers neither consolation nor despair. 'No nearer Jerusalem ... Unapproachable City of God', he notes in *Speech! Speech!* (117). But just as he will not submit to the materialist determinisms of 'Destiny' or 'History'; nor find comfort in being subsumed into the innocence of Averroes's 'Idea', the attraction of which he registers in 'Funeral Music'; neither can he subscribe to the strongest versions of predestination, 'guaranteed / damnation for dead children unbaptized' and the rest (*TL* CXXV, p. 67).

This, I think, is for two reasons. First, he cannot sustain such *contemptus mundi* in the face of the sensuous beauty of the world. This appears in erotic pleasure in such work as 'The Songbook of Sebastian Arrurruz' (*King Log*; *CP* pp. 92-102); in the perpetual fascination with wordplay; in comedy as honoured – Laurel and Hardy's 'flawless shambles' in *The Triumph of Love* – and imitated – Frankie Howerd, 'Be serious' (*Syon* XXXIX) and others in *Speech! Speech!*: 'Look on the bright side. WHÁDDYA – WHÁDDYA – / call thís – script or prescription?' (*SpSp* 107);[10] and in the flowers, plants, clouds, changing light that are so marked in the later volumes. There *is* something of Syon in this world.

The second seems more baleful. 'Nothing is unforgettable but guilt', he writes in *Scenes from Comus* (3.19); 'I am ashamed and grieve' ('Pisgah'). What religious thought gives is the conviction of being beholden, accountable, and with that the notion of agency, of being responsible. Each might have been a 'difficult friend', but Hill admires those such as Mandelstam, Péguy, Von Haeften, Bonhoeffer, Okigbo who choose and act, daring the dangers of 'wilfulness and determination' (*TL* CXXXIX, p. 75). As one acutely aware of his own failings, and, as against these exemplars, one who must say 'I have not been there', the restless question is how would I compare?

heroic / verse a non-starter, says *PEOPLE* (*Speech! Speech*! 1)

Can any of these obligations be discharged through the poet's task? Is it possible that poetry today can be 'a bit of real matter lodged in the body politic' (*LL* p. 143)? Can it be 'performative'?

One dimension of Hill's work that has become more evident in the later work has been his self-conscious use of the rhetorical modes of *laus et vituperatio* – praise and vituperation. Both what he admires and deplores is especially marked throughout *Canaan*, *The Triumph of Love* and *Speech! Speech!* They, and the character of their expression, might be summarised in one of the several addresses 'in absentia' included in *Canaan*, the one to William Cobbett, which closes,

> your righteous unjust and cordial anger,
> your singular pitch where labour is spoken of,
> your labour that brought to pass
> reborn Commodity with uplifted hands
> awed by its own predation
>
> (*Cn* p. 9)

Anger is always something paradoxical, hence 'righteous unjust'. It can be 'righteous' but its energy will generate force which will carry it beyond justice with a warmth exceeding the normal bounds of cordiality. This is one of the difficulties of expression and shows how the oxymoron is so significant a figure in compressing the experience of this kind of contradiction. The shapeliness of oxymoron can exert its own excessive attraction, but it does enact the real complexity of attitude and opinion. But the conviction of Cobbett's that Hill certainly rests upon is his perception that wealth comes from labour, from 'the three hundred thousand little girls in Lancashire' as Cobbett memorably told Parliament,[11] from 'the nailer's darg'. Only in the substance of these lives can we recognise value. But the helpless hypocrisy of those 'uplifted hands' (in horror or in prayer?) will seem impotent before modern 'Commodity'. Where in the speech of the world can such a voice of protest be heard? 'Savage indignation' can become a capering, an archaic ritual, a 'dance with antlers' as the fourth poem of 'Cycle' has it (*Cn* p. 39). Cobbett, Bunyan, Wesley in *Canaan* join the ranks of Hill's against-the-grain, practically defeated heroes, like Péguy: 'Outflanked again, too bad!' (4). The late Roy Porter, in his paean to modernity, dubs its critics and sceptics a company of 'dogged self-marginalizers like Swift, Wesley and Blake'.[12] It is a company that would readily recognise Hill, and one I think he would be proud to own.

But the poet's efficacy is not to be measured in daily persuasion. I have been arguing throughout this essay that Hill's struggle for 'acceptable words' is one which tries to find expression commensurate with the strong subjects that compel him; words that will not take advantage of the grace of 'moral luck' but do justice; words that are wrought from the infinite extent and complexity of contemporary language and its indelible histories; words that will combine the immediate with the mediate, 'the intellective with the sensuous elements of language' (*RV* p. 277). Failure in this struggle is easy: 'the distance between grace and sentiment may be the breadth of a syllable, dissolved in an instant' (*Style and Faith*, p. 127). The task is 'getting it right', and for Hill that is an ethical task, a paradigm for the greater tasks and complexities of life.[13]

Hill's poem in memory of Ken Smith, 'Carnal Policy', published in *Stand* in Spring 2005,[14] begins with the limits of poetry:

> Hazardous but press on. Enjambment
> drags: hinge of induration
> not a patent success.

As in Bunyan's town Carnal Policy, there are snares and delusions: 'Not everything's a joke but we've been had.' In the second part the poem tries to press through 'the province / of human discourse, error, self-delusion', though the way seems blocked:

> Unexchangeable password, I have yet
> to find the place appointed. It will come.
>
> Over, across, the Pennine scarps and valleys
> motorway lights – festal suspension bridge,
> high-arching nocturne. I grasp the possible
>
> rightness of certain things
> that possess the imagination, however briefly;
>
> the verdict of their patterned randomness.

The 'rightness', especially in the latest work, is seen in these moments of intensity of being, even in the commonest things. The achievement of their realisation in words and so in memory resists oblivion. None the less there will not be a last word.

2 'The speechless dead': *King Log* (1968)

The battle at Shiloh Church, fought over two days in April 1862, ended with the slaughter accomplished of thirteen thousand Federal soldiers and ten thousand Confederates. It was the greatest battle fought on the American continent up to that date. A chromolithograph, reproduced in Bruce Catton's *The Penguin Book of the American Civil War*,[1] shows the two sides fighting it out at point- blank range amid a wilderness of carnage. The impression is of a holocaust so locking the combatants that none will move without the achievement of total destruction, their own as well as their enemies'. Behind the ranks of federal riflemen, apparently impassive on their horses, the officers sit determined to see the events to their full completion:

> O stamping-ground of the shod Word! So hard
> On the heels of the damned red-man we came,
> Geneva's tribe, outlandish and abhorred –
> Bland vistas milky with Jehovah's calm –
>
> Who fell to feasting Nature, the glare
> Of buzzards circling; cried to the grim sun
> 'Jehovah punish us!'
>
> ('Locust Songs', *CP* p. 65)

The presentation of such a tableau as this at Shiloh Church, or the Battle of Towton almost exactly four hundred years earlier under the comet's light in 'Funeral Music', appears as a central feature of *King Log*. Such single revelations haunt Hill's imagination. They act as images that compound his obsession with human suffering, 'circumstantial disasters', and all that compromises those circumstances – the condition and posture of the suffering, the façade, the imaginings and, most of all, those who contemplate.

Such contemplation is not a new aspect of Hill's work. Aware as always, of the reprehensible dangers of affectation and cheapness in contemplating the dead, he wrote in *For the Unfallen*, published in 1959:

> Some of us have heard the dead speak:
> The dead are my obsession this week
>
> But may be lifted away.
> ('Of Commerce and Society' 4, *CP* p. 49)

No sooner has the speaker pretended to visionary knowledge than the claim is undermined, trashed even, by a scepticism that sees it as an affectation, or something like a nervous headache, readily relieved even when inflated as the lifting away of care. This wariness is accompanied by a tremendous sense in *For the Unfallen* of the sheer physical fact of death, the total erasure of a human being. The fourth poem in the 'Metamorphoses' sequence, 'Drake's Drum', is only one example:

> Those varied dead. The undiscerning sea
> Shelves and dissolves their flesh as it burns spray[.]
> (*CP* p. 35)

The ordinary sense of 'shelve', of 'put away', 'dispose of', is here brilliantly linked with the evocative physical sense of the ledges of the sea-bottom at work upon the corpse. Such a use of language, as Christopher Ricks demonstrated in his valuable article on Hill's work 'Cliché as Responsible Speech',[2] is a vital characteristic of his work. Here as with the empty sleeve and shoe washed ashore later in the poem, it is the concreteness of the image, its ability to occupy the imagination, that ensures its success. Hill begins from the *fact* of death, compels the reader's comprehension of its emptiness and is then appalled at the indifferent resumption of the external world, as in these lines evoking Towton after the battle:

> Reddish ice tinged the reeds; dislodged, a few
> Feathers drifted across; carrion birds
> Strutted upon the armour of the dead.
> ('Funeral Music' 7; *CP* p. 76)

More than indifference, the birds' strut even suggests nature's mockery of human pretension, of their *amour propre* as of their armour. Hill's concern is with what is spoken as we focus our uneasy gaze on 'the smitten man'.

This attention in *King Log* centres very much on the public world. The epigraph to the volume's 1968 edition is from Bacon's *The Advancement of Learning* – 'From moral virtue let us pass on to matter of power and commandment' – and the title (from Aesop's fable of the frogs who rejected the log Zeus gave them as king only to be eaten by his successor a water snake) points towards an intermittent theme of ironic and bitter contemplation of the respective dignities of ruler and ruled. The dead of Towton and the surrounding slaughter on the state-executioner's block and elsewhere; the dead of Shiloh; the victims of the Third Reich; the four poets Campanella, Hernandez, Desnos and Mandelstam, victims of the Counter-Reformation, Franco, the Nazis and Stalinism respectively, all these are the matter of 'power and commandment' which has 'passed on' from moral virtue. All are public victims, crushed by force that must seem as implacable and deterministic as that represented by the shelving sea or the strutting crow. But the human world of 'power and commandment' is not in fact associated with these. It is instead a world which includes responsibility and choice.

This area of possibility, the options of behaviour available to human beings, are often discussed by Hill in terms of the myth of the Fall, a major emblem for him, but only one part of the Western religious mythology which can be used as an imaginative framework and scheme of reference for the paradoxes and ambiguities he sees in the human situation. The three parts of 'Locust Songs' lead up to Shiloh Church in terms of the early American vision of the New World as a new Eden:

> So with sweet oaths converting the salt earth
> To yield, our fathers verged on Paradise:
> Each to his own portion of Paradise,
> Stung by the innocent venoms of the earth.
> (CP p. 64)

The destruction of this ideal in a locust-like falling upon that land, is compounded by the tortuous Calvinistic confusion of worldly greed and lust for the wrath of an implacable God, 'writhing over the rich scene', so that Shiloh is seeking

> God in this
> His natural filth, voyeur of sacrifice, a slow
> Bloody unearthing of the God-in-us.

Their Paradise was a fallen world, and seeking evidence of their own election, God within them, they created Hell. As in that tumultuous poem which opens Hill's published work, 'Genesis', the question is whether the 'God-in-us' is mild or bloody, ravage or redemption (CP pp. 15–16). In the second sonnet of 'Funeral Music' one of the three beheaded aristocrats asks:

> For whom do we scrape our tribute of pain –
> For none but the ritual king? We meditate
> A rueful mystery[.]
>
> (*CP* p. 71)

The justification of pain, and so of the whole fallen world, is open to rejection. The 'ritual king' may mean the earthly monarch as opposed to the real king who is God, though might he too be no more than 'ritual'? The word 'mystery' has connotations not just of 'problem' but of a secret religious doctrine, a possibility that is beyond human knowledge to explain, as well as the further meaning of 'anything artfully made difficult'. The vision of 'all reconciled / By silent music' is elusive. Such careful planning of a fallen world towards 'Ultimate recompense' cannot be made consistent with the evident arbitrariness of human suffering. The poem concludes:

> Acres, parched, sodden or blanched by sleet,
> Stuck with strange-postured dead. Recall the wind's
> Flurrying, darkness over the human mire.

Yet elsewhere the apparently arbitrary can be seen to be manipulated with a fearful control. To the 'innocent' German of 'Ovid in the Third Reich' the world outside his small control seems impossible, incomprehensible:

> I love my work and my children. God
> Is distant, difficult. Things happen.
> Too near the ancient troughs of blood
> Innocence is no earthly weapon.
>
> (*CP* p. 61)

'Things happen' out of a whirling, untenable space, a void. But there is still a moral imperative. The worldly epigraph from Ovid's *Amores* – '*non peccat, quaecumquae potest pecasse negare, / solaque famosam culpa professa facit*', essentially 'whoever can deny wrongdoing is innocent; only those who own up are guilty' – points towards the invidiousness of quietism under the Third Reich. A similar impersonality appears to overhang the fate of the Jewish child of 'September Song *born 19.6.32 – deported 24.9.42*':

> Not forgotten
> or passed over at the proper time.
>
> As estimated, you died. Things marched,
> sufficient, to that end.
> Just so much Zyklon and leather, patented
> terror, so many routine cries.
>
> (*CP* p. 67)

'Things marched', but all is calculated, precisely organised. Things are rationalised so that this time the Jews are not passed over. And in this world of power and commandment, where knowledge can be put to such use, neither the child's pristine innocence nor moral virtue is of any help. Instead 'undesirable', with its suggestion of 'undesirable alien', and 'untouchable' imply violation. In juxtaposing the child's condition in 'September Song' with his own autumnal comfort – 'This is plenty. This is more than enough' – Hill is also pointing towards a corruption of language where such words as 'sufficient', 'plenty' and 'enough' can be used indeterminately to disguise what they are quantitative of: 'The Minister assured the House that sufficient is being done.' How much resonance such a word can carry might be illustrated by these words from Defoe's *A Tour thro' Great Britain* on encountering the child-workers in the wool cottage industry near Halifax in the early eighteenth century: 'All can gain their bread, even from the youngest to the antient; hardly anything above four years old, but its hands are sufficient to it self ...' Such seismic sensitivity to the language as Hill here displays demands of course that he be equally aware of the vulnerability of his own language. He is aware of how his regarding of the dead child can become an indulgence:

> (I have made
> an elegy for myself it
> is true)

The poem itself is a luxury, a part of the plenty, the leisure of refining line-breaks, of making the tremendously delicate association of the smoke of autumn's garden bonfire with that from the ovens of Auschwitz or Treblinka:

> September fattens on vines. Roses
> flake from the wall. The smoke
> of harmless fires drifts to my eyes.
>
> This is plenty. This is more than enough.

The poet cannot be merely indignant but must recognise the ethical implication that comes just through knowledge and its acknowledgement. That is compounded by the act of writing a poem, something always done for oneself – 'I have made an elegy for myself' – but the problem must be reckoned with in every kind of representation. 'September Song' is an honouring of the child who is the poet's own exact contemporary but it is also 'about' this problem. The poem is appalled by the 'things' that happen to make two different lives, and humbled by the unavoidable provisionality of the expression itself. Good intentions alone are inadequate, virtuous rhetoric fraught with the perils of glibness, the Word made fashionable as in 'Annunciations':

> The Word has been abroad, is back, with a tanned look
> From its subsistence in the stiffening-mire,
>
> (*CP* p. 62)

and in 'The Humanist':

> the achieved guest
> Tired and word-perfect
> At the Muses' table.
>
> (*CP* p. 69)

Hill's humanist's regard for words is of a kind with his regard for food – 'A delicate white meat' – and Hill's criticism of it might be compared to that comment of Wordsworth's in the *Preface* where he inveighs against those who speak of their 'taste' for poetry much as they might of their taste 'for Rope-dancing or Frontiniac or Sherry'.[3]

For Hill all expression seems akin to indulgence, the over-articulate serpent offering the apple of garrulity. Yet silence is impossible:

> Words clawed my mind as though they had smelt
>
> Revelation's flesh ... So, with an ease
> That is dreadful, I summon all back.
>
> ('Soliloquies', *CP* p. 85)

King Log is at war with such ease, indeed with the rich verbal command its poet can muster. Commonly spoken of as a 'gift', it is more than gratuitous, especially when referred to as 'divine'. The imagery of men mocked by doubtful divine gifts is one that recurs through the book, most particularly with regard to the seraphic Pentecostal touch of the gift of tongues: 'taste / Of Pentecost's ashen feast' ('History as Poetry', *CP* p. 84). The peace, or silence, which Campanella would have in 'Men Are a Mockery of Angels' is momentary, and seen as such:

> To lie here in my strange
> Flesh while glutted Torment
> Sleeps, stained with its prompt food,
> Is a joy past all care
> Of the world, for a time.
> But we are commanded
> To rise, when, in silence,
> I would compose my voice.
>
> (*CP* p. 78)

The whole effort is towards composure that is at the same time compo-sition. Those first five lines are a beautiful utterance, powerfully imag-ined – 'stained with its prompt food' – and the cadence is perfectly managed to rise through the run-on line to the ecstasy of a 'joy past all care / Of the world' and die with the matter-of-fact qualification 'for a time'. Very often Hill adapts familiar stanza forms and apparently even lines to disrupt expectation, here employing strong, irregular stress in six syllable lines together with abrupt enjambments: 'To **lie here** in my **strange / Flesh** …'.

'Funeral Music', a sequence of eight fourteen-line poems that arises out of contemplation of episodes from the Wars of the Roses, is accom-panied by a short essay commenting on and illuminating some aspects of the background (*CP* pp. 199–201). In this Hill writes of the poems as 'attempting a florid grim music broken by grunts and shrieks'. The bro-kenness is first signalled by the fact that although the series looks to invite the description of a sonnet sequence, it is unrhymed and follows none of the accepted internal patterns. In his essay 'Vers Libre and Arnold Dolmetsch', Ezra Pound writes of 'Couperin's feeling for irregularity underlying "classical" forms'.[4] This is what we hear in 'Funeral Music' through Hill's contortions of the form and by his pressing the tension between sound and silence.

> A field
> After battle utters its own sound
> Which is like nothing on earth, but is earth.
> Blindly the questing snail, vulnerable
> Mole emerge, blindly we lie down, blindly
> Among carnage the most delicate souls
> Tup in their marriage-blood, gasping 'Jesus'.
>
> (3, *CP* p. 72)

These mainly ten-syllable lines eschew the iambic as they feel their way with the silent snail and mole from the battlefield, first haltingly, even without any commas after 'field' and 'sound', then moving onwards to this astonishing and horrific summation of human action in which the bloodletting of warfare and the nuptial bed are conflated, even for the most 'delicate souls', into an animalistic orgasmic shudder and cry. If the thinking protagonists of the sequence – or we – could see past this, as Campanella briefly imagines, 'past all care / Of the world', then it might be borne as without consequence as in the theology of Averroes which saw not the individually accountable immortal soul but a merged eter-nity of 'Intellect':

> Averroes, old heathen,
> If only you had been right, if Intellect
> Itself were absolute law, sufficient grace,
> Our lives could be a myth of captivity
> Which we might enter: an unpeopled region
> Of ever new-fallen snow, a palace blazing
> With perpetual silence as with torches.[5]
>
> (4, *CP* p. 73)

But it cannot be so annealed. Such an eternity would indeed be 'unpeopled' and the human world is ineluctably marked by an unsettled confusion of sufferings and brutality. There are gestures of some kind of defiance such as Tiptoft's request to be beheaded in three strokes in honour of the Trinity; and a few men such as Suffolk and Rivers searching out some small area to suffer their contemplation. But there is no silence, instead, at every turn, the 'whining Psalteries', the trumpets, 'wild Christmas' and its revel of 'atonement'. The Peaceable Kingdom, the child's glimpse, is already reached by 'The world's real cries'. So, finally, in the eighth poem:

> If it is without
> Consequence when we vaunt and suffer, or
> If it is not, all echoes are the same
> In such eternity. Then tell me, love,
> How that should comfort us – or anyone
> Dragged half-unnerved out of this worldly place,
> Crying to the end 'I have not finished'.
>
> (*CP* p. 77)

It is another desperate ejaculation but it would be a defeat to lapse into numbed silence. No rationalisation, no nihilism, no consolation, can render death acceptable.

It would however be a mistake to parcel this into an abstract and transportable conclusion of 'Funeral Music'. It is a particular culmination. The last poem in *King Log*, the eleventh and final poem of 'The Songbook of Sebastian Arrurruz' – the apocryphal Spanish poet to whom Hill has given the dates 1868–1922 – appears from its statement to be a retreat towards silence:

> Scarcely speaking: it becomes as a
> Coolness between neighbours. Often
> There is this orgy of sleep. I wake
> To caress propriety with odd words
> And enjoy abstinence in a vocation
> Of now-almost-meaningless despair.
>
> (*CP* p. 102)

But in context this is the dying fall in a movement of poems concerning the loss of love and the writing of poems. The poem is the sounding, or imagining, of a last despair, a poem pretending that a tired skill has no more interest now in its practice than to write a poem in which each line occupies the same amount of type-space. The phrase 'now-almost-meaningless' is hyphenated to point up its accession into cliché, though a cliché restored to hint at the real despair of the poet which is the possibility that, because of the contraction of valid speech, he is no longer able to say anything meaningful. It is another aspect of the dubiety with which Hill can regard poetry. The first Arrurruz poem asserts its value, a definite assertion, but even so is not wholly free of a certain over-deliberateness, a self conscious stiffness:

> For so it is proper to find value
> In a bleak skill, as in the thing restored[.]
> (*CP* p. 92)

It is as though, whilst making the statement, he is allowing for the moments when he is less certain. Characteristically, Hill seeks to include each modulation of thought and feeling present in his contemplation of his subject.

> The exact words
>
> Are fed into my blank hunger for you.
> (5, *CP* p. 96)

'The exact words' are Geoffrey Hill's total concern as a poet. His determination is to strive to make them adequate to the events he witnesses. *King Log* is fruit of that witness and that determination. For its enhancement of our witness, and of our sense and feeling for the language we use, it commands admiration.

> Poetry as salutation; taste
> Of Pentecost's ashen feast. Blue wounds.
> The tongue's atrocities. Poetry
> Unearths from among the speechless dead
>
> Lazarus mystified, common man
> Of death.
> ('History as Poetry', *CP* p. 84)

3 Poet, lover, liar: 'Lachrimae' (1975)

Robert Southwell (1561–95), Catholic martyr and poet from whose work Geoffrey Hill takes his epigraph for his 1975 sonnet sequence 'Lachrimae or Seven tears figured in seven passionate Pavans' (*Tenebrae*, 1978; *CP* pp. 145–51) wrote in his posthumous work *St Peter's Complaint* (1595) of what he saw as his contemporaries' abuse of their poetic talents: 'a poet, a lover and a liar are by many reckoned but three things with one signification'. That the identification of poetry and feigning was nearly a commonplace in Elizabethan literary culture might be gauged by its reiteration by the rather less spiritually inclined Touchstone in *As You Like It* (Act III, Scene 3), and in the kindred formulation in Sidney's *Apologie*, 'the poet never lieth for he nothing affirmeth', an assertion Hill uses as a basis for his pondering of poetry and truth in the essay 'Our Word Is Our Bond' (*LL* pp. 138–59). 'Lachrimae' is a 'religious' work in that it twitches the mantle of devotional verse, but it also explores the nature of the discourse of religion by both adopting and parodying its traditional figures and vocabulary. Through this the sequence searches the unfathomable conundrum of poetry, and, by extension, the other arts, indeed language itself: the relationship between expression and the truth of thought and feeling. This traditionally formal sequence is deliberately stately, but, in the imitation it employs, the spirit of Touchstone is not wholly absent either. For now however, let us stay with Southwell.

The impatience in *St Peter's Complaint* with the worldliness of contemporary poets is consistent with the indifference to earthly life to which Southwell and his fellow missionary martyrs aspired throughout their training and work. At the English College in Rome he had lived beneath the paintings of the horrendous sufferings of his predecessors at the hands of Elizabeth's government: a true art in his eyes. Southwell longed not only for death but for the utmost suffering to attain his martyr's crown. Living in a world of suffering and misery he sought the apotheosis of that suffering. The historian A. O. Meyer describes Southwell by the time of his execution in 1595 as

A citizen of the other world who delights in renouncing this world,
and feels nothing but compassion for those deluded people to
whom all things are not yet vain and empty.
Life is but loss– I die alive – at home in heaven –
are the favourite themes of his poems.[1]

It is as though in seeking his crown he redefines life, distils it to an essence
consisting only of the finely considered point of pain devised by his torturer.
The artful inventiveness of Richard Topcliffe MP, a man who seems to have
been so absorbed by the sensations of human flesh, is to be the instrument
of that achievement. It will be a transcendence like that of Tommaso
Campanella in Hill's earlier poem. 'Men Are a Mockery of Angels':

> a joy past all care
> Of the world, for a time.
> (*CP* p. 78)

But – only 'for a time'. Is it possible to so annihilate the world? The
purest transcendence is lapped by some part of sensuous life, and
Southwell protested in court (as how could he not?) at his being tortured,
and at the inflicting of pain as an accoutrement of state policy. Then there
is love, human and sensual – 'clamorous love' as Hill has it, taking a lively
risk with that pun. And always too, especially because the martyr is making
– *composing* – his life, there is the ambush of contrivance of some sort, and
any design is obliged to partake of earthly existence and its sophisticated
ironies. This last is a major theme in the 'Lachrimae' sequence, most devel-
oped in the fifth sonnet, 'Pavana Dolorosa'. There Hill works on his epi-
graph from Southwell's *Mary Magdalens Funeral Teares*:

> Passions I allow, and loves I approve, onely
> I would wishe that men would alter their
> object and better their intent.

He inverts the first phrase of the epigraph, turning words over in the
manner of a reply by the jesters Touchstone or Feste, and so faintly satiris-
ing Southwell's naive if winning concession:

> Loves I allow and passions I approve:
> Ash-Wednesday feasts, ascetic opulence,
> the wincing lute, so real in its pretence,
> itself a passion amorous of love.
>
> Self- wounding martyrdom, what joys you have,
> true-torn among this fictive consonance,
> ('Pavana Dolorosa', *CP* p. 149)

The poem works the word 'passion' to show how its ostensibly very different meanings are inextricable. Concentration upon 'Passion' in the sense of suffering trial, as in 'the passion of Christ', shades into indulgence in the oxymoron 'ascetic opulence'. The implications of amorous passion associate it with the flesh it seeks to deny, and in searching out his passion the martyr is wounding himself; in mocking up his own passion he is making a mockery of it. In celebrating the 'joys' of martyrdom, the voice parodies itself to a degree in that the quest for martyrdom becomes almost a virtuoso performance, a form, an art work in itself,

> Self-seeking hunter of forms, there is no end
> to such pursuits. None can revoke your cry.
> Your silence is an ecstasy of sound
>
> and your nocturnals blaze upon the day.

The climax of the martyr's cry is so perfect it is silence. Since its achievement is death, it is art so perfect as to be beyond art. An analogy might be Kretschmar's description in Thomas Mann's *Doctor Faustus* when he speaks of

> music's deepest wish not to be heard at all, nor even
> seen, nor yet felt: but only – if that were possible – in
> some Beyond, the other side of sense and sentiment, to
> be perceived and contemplated as pure mind, pure spirit.[2]

The sound that is no sound is one of the several paradoxes here and elsewhere in the sequence – 'ascetic opulence', 'real in its pretence', 'the moveless dance' and the posed final lines:

> I founder in desire for things unfound.
> I stay amid the things that will not stay.

Paradox seems to recur in the sensibility of martyrdom: Southwell 'I die alive'; San Juan de la Cruz (evoked by Hill in another sequence 'The Pentecost Castle', *CP* 137–44) speaks of 'dying of not dying'. The martyr's progress to find utmost joy in suffering, life in death, lives a paradox. It is appropriate, but paradox has a neatness, a shapeliness which is seductive and might betray. In such abnegation as the martyr seeks, 'self-wounding' might yet be 'self-seeking'. The world is not so readily transcended or even evaded. The pious figure in the next poem, 'Martyrium', is 'Jesus-faced'. Uncomfortably and deliberately close to 'Janus-faced', he looks both ways.

The image here which – *as* a representation – most exemplifies such paradox and complexity is the crucifixion, the 'Crucified Lord' who is the

sequence's primary addressee. In the first poem, 'Lachrimae Verae', the
persona cannot see Christ as what belief should tell him he is: 'you swim
upon your cross / and never move', where 'move' is a pun, neither moving
himself nor moving the spectator. Instead Christ is 'our' construct:

> This is your body twisted by our skill
> into a patience proper for redress.

Christ's body is given back to him, twisted perhaps literally as in a cruci-
fixion such as Grünewald's tortured painting, but also fixed by human
device, our own image for our own reproach, bearable and indeed beau-
tiful as in this perfect and euphonious iambic pentameter: 'You are the
castaway of drowned remorse'. Christ's image should show the essential
truth, but we are seduced elsewhere, into the beauty of the artefact, the
sensuous world. Perhaps the dreamy martyr, that 'Jesus-faced man',
might be immune but he has become an ever more distant, aestheticised
figure, fading 'among the fading tapestries' and cannot help us:

> Clamorous love, its faint and baffled shout,
> its grief that would betray him to our fear,
> he suffers for our sake, or does not hear
>
> above the hiss of shadows on the wheat.

> (3)

To the martyr's sensibility the vision of earthly life is quintessentially one
of suffering. Art might, if it can attain some sort of brilliant purity, express
this, but more often its sensuousness will only divert. This is the criticism
that the voices of the first three of Hill's sonnets present, not only argued
but embodied in their own elegant formal disposition:

> Viaticum transfigures earth's desire
> in rising vernicles of summer air.

> (3)

So the poet might be said to be undermining his own vocation. The
master of figures reveals nothing but his own process of transfiguration.
The rigour of such a critique of art and reality is also pursued by Geoffrey
Hill in an essay called '"The Conscious Mind's Intelligible Structure", a
Debate'.[3] Here he takes considered issue with Czeslaw Milosz and what
he calls Milosz's 'new terms of the utmost purity: things and moments'
which will always, writes Milosz, '*judge* all poets and philosophers'. We
find a kindred discussion of how art and the world outside art relate in
Herbert Marcuse's *An Essay on Liberation*. First Marcuse eloquently
describes the claims of art:

The aesthetic necessity of art supersedes the terrible necessity of
reality, sublimates its pain and pleasure; the blind suffering and cru-
elty of nature (and of the 'nature' of man) assume meaning and end
– 'poetic justice'. The horror of the crucifixion is purified by the
beautiful fact of Jesus dominating the beautiful composition, the
horror of politics by the beautiful verse of Racine, the horror of
farewell for ever by the *Lied von der Erde*. And in this aesthetic uni-
verse, joy and fulfilment find their proper place alongside pain and
death – everything is in order again.

Then reality returns,

> the achievement is illusory, false, fictitious: it remains within the
> dimension of art, a work of art ... This is perhaps the most telling
> expression of the contradiction, the self-defeat, built into art: the
> pacifying conquest of matter, the transfiguration of the object
> remain unreal – just as the revolution in perception remains unreal.[4]

'This is your body twisted by our skill / into a patience proper for redress.'

The reason I have sought to indicate some of the historical back-
ground suggested in 'Lachrimae', and by the reference to Robert
Southwell in particular, is because for all their apparent esotericism these
poems do live in history. The sonnets are oblique and do not deal with
'things and moments' even as directly as does Hill's earlier 'Funeral
Music', but the matter of history, the world of sensuousness and of suf-
fering is always at hand. The second poem, 'The Masque of Blackness',
presents it in a self-consciously distanced way which touches parody in
its consideration of the attractiveness of the material world:

> Splendour of life so splendidly contained,
> brilliance made bearable. It is the east
> light's embodiment, fit to be caressed,
> the god Amor with his eyes of diamond,
>
> celestial worldliness on which has dawned
> intelligence of angels, Midas' feast,
> the stony hunger of the dispossessed
> locked into Eden by their own demand.

'The god Amor' has a much more palpably sensual existence in Hill's
'The Songbook of Sebastian Arrurruz' in *King Log*: 'my tongue in your
furrow', 'your hand over me like a sinew of water' – love there is more
clamorous. But the difference from the stricken Arrurruz is that here the
masquer, or philosopher, is organising experience, 'mastering' the world
through his articulate contriving. The very articulateness of the verse

shows that these qualities are valued, though again they are almost imme-
diately undermined when that claimed mastery of the material world is
given a more sinister association in the sudden and perfectly delicate tac-
tile image:

> Midas' feast,
> the stony hunger of the dispossessed[.]

'The stony hunger of the dispossessed', brilliantly merging the ideas of
Midas's feast and the Sermon on the Mount – 'if his son ask bread, will
he give him a stone, – strikes hard through the insouciance of this
'masque'. The linguistic depth of this particular sonnet is amazing, as is
the sureness of its pitch and movement, especially in the sestet:

> Self-love, the slavish master of this trade,
> conquistador of fashion and remark,
> models new heavens in his masquerade,
>
> its images intense with starry work,
> until he tires and all that he has made
> vanishes in the chaos of the dark.

Myriad human activity, the intricacy of our artefacts (including such a
complex and formal poem as this) carried in those words 'intense with
starry work' – we are dazzling! – then evaporates, first in the bored sigh
of the caesura after 'until he tires', and then as the last line settles on 'van-
ishes' with a clap of the hands in that first syllable stress.

It is at this point in discussing the artifice, and the matter of artifice,
in 'Lachrimae' that I want to consider their model, John Dowland's own
'Lachrimae', 'seven passionate pavans'. The pavan is a slow, stately, grave
dance, the dancers elaborately dressed, proving the contradiction
between the 'splendour of life' and a sense of its tragic movement, a slow-
ness aspiring towards the motionlessness that human beings ultimately
achieve, 'the moveless dance, / the decreation to which all must move'
('Pavana Dolorosa'). Here, in a medieval elaboration of symbolism, each
pavan is a tear, a tiny globe, and the number seven, unspokenly, that of
the seven ages. So the world and human life is self-consciously formu-
lated. Hill plays off these associations of studied Elizabethan melancholy
as Dowland himself did to judge from the implied self-satire in his pun-
ning signature 'Jo: dolandi de Lachrimae', and of another of his works
'Semper Dowland. Semper dolens'. It is just such hints at Dowland's sen-
sibility which must reinforce Hill's attraction to his music, so sensible
himself of the utility of puns and verbal play: 'the wincing lute, so real in
its pretence, / itself a passion amorous of love'. But more than that is the

association that Hill is properly making between Dowland's music and the sensuous quality of his own verse. Dowland's biographer and expositor Diana Poulton writes of the composer's 'constant search for the exact expression of sadness and melancholy',[5] and it is that quality of *exact* expression which Hill seeks and achieves, matching the delicacy and precision of Dowland's music. There is I believe an affinity too with how we might relate Dowland's work to the world in which it was composed. Dowland, whose melancholy might well it seems have been both real and studied, had before him not only the routine brevity and brutality of life in sixteenth- and seventeenth- century Europe, but particularly the oppression of his fellow Catholics in England, of whom Southwell was one. Obviously simplistic biographical 'explanations' are not what is interesting here. What is clear however from the music is that the sadness of 'Lachrimae' is no mere exercise. Yet what can it *say* with its wordlessness? One answer might come from one point of view put forward for rejection by Marcuse in the passage from *An Essay on Liberation* already referred to where he writes of 'the redeeming, reconciling power of art', its purification and sublimation of reality created by 'the aesthetic necessity' of the *oeuvre*. Marcuse is surely right to be suspicious of such regular spiritual triumph, and for an example of such redemption we might turn, as Hill does in the sixth sonnet 'Lachrimae Antiquae Novae', to the habitual observances of the Christian church.

> Beautiful for themselves the icons fade;
> the lions and the hermits disappear.
> Triumphalism feasts on empty dread,
>
> fulfilling triumphs of the festal year.
> We find you wounded by the token spear.
> Dominion is swallowed with your blood.

The beauty of religious imagery is purely aesthetic, but the phrase 'for themselves' also suggests that they are turned inwards. The rituals of Christianity become celebrations from which its message of pain has been evacuated. The blood of Christ in the eucharist becomes blood in the mouth of the defeated. The self-regard, self-absorption, of forms can make them heartless, even complicit in the order of suffering. Here we might see what Marcuse calls 'the self-defeat, built into art'. Yet in this complex time, whilst we still only anticipate the whole developed liberation in which Marcuse, like Mann's Adrian Leverkuhn, will see the 'end' of art, when we 'will not have a culture but will perhaps be a culture',[6] artifice, even cunning, Hill would say,[7] seems unavoidable if we are to say anything, or moreover, as the martyr's gesture suggests, perhaps even if we are

to do anything. These poems do not and do pretend to cancel the indict-
ment of the suffering world outside art. They are a piteous and pitiful
accompaniment to that reality. They are also a profound discussion and
demonstration of artifice in expression. Truly it is a dangerous game. Our
language has woven the several connotations around the words 'artifice'
and 'artificial' for good reasons. Hill acknowledges his involvement not
least in his references and evocations of earlier practitioners: Dowland,
Peter Phillips, Quevedo, Lope de Vega – guilt by association. In
'Lachrimae' the image of Christ on the cross serves as the most powerful
emblem of suffering, the central fact of human existence, and shows the
difficulty, even impossibility, of seeing this through the representation.
The last poem of the sequence is a working of a sonnet by Lope de Vega
'Qué tengo yo que mi amistad procuras?',[8] the last lines of which are:

> So many nights the angel of my house
> has fed such urgent comfort through a dream,
> whispered 'your lord is coming, he is close'
>
> that I have drowsed half-faithful for a time
> bathed in pure tones of promise and remorse:
> 'tomorrow I shall wake to welcome him'.

Of course it would be preferable to be straightforward and sincere, to be
instantly and truly struck by the real, and to be able just to say, with
George Herbert in 'The Collar, '*My Lord!*'

4 'Our love is what we love to have': *Tenebrae* (1978)

Geoffrey Hill's poems have often presented us with a series of scenes, livid tableaux, 'spectacles': the Jews in Europe, the Battle of Towton, the endurances of some poets, Boethius in his cell, the nailer's darg, real and fancied martyrdoms like those of his Sebastians. If his vision of the world were to be put in symbolic terms then the character of the Romanesque style as described by Henri Focillon might provide an analogy:

> Romanesque art had perceived [all created things] only through a mesh of ornament and in a monstrous disguise. It had combined man with beast and beast with Chimera. It had festooned the capitals of churches with a fantastic menagerie, and stamped the tympana of churches with the seal of the Apocalypse. The very profusion and variety of these incessantly metamorphosed beings betray the impatience of their struggle to break out from the labyrinth of abstract style and to achieve life. It seems, not the created world, but the dream of God on the eve of Creation, a terrible first draft of his plan. It is the encyclopaedia of the imagination, preceding the encyclopaedia of reality.[1]

The 'festooning' of Romanesque is evoked in *Mercian Hymns* (*CP* pp. 103–34): 'I wormed my way heavenward for | ages amid barbaric ivy, scrollwork of fern' (V); in tapestry: 'voluted grape-vine, master- | works of treacherous thread' (XXIII); and in the master-mason of Hymn XXIV who comes home from Compostela

> intent to pester upon tympanum and chancel-
> arch his moody testament, confusing warrior with
> lion, dragon-coils, tendrils of the stony vine.

The 'spectacles' may be frozen and sometimes unbearably bright, but they are not ordered or illuminated by a clear humanist vision, by reason, or by consoling Christianity. But their world is endlessly fecund. It can be a blind animalised thriving of copulation upon an earth of sickly richness imagined in such poems from *King Log* as 'Annunciations' – 'the loathly neckings' (*CP* p. 62), and 'The Imaginative Life' (*CP* p. 82). Perhaps the most vivid feature of *Mercian Hymns* is the child-narrator's eye and nose-level sense of vegetation and the bodily world: 'tacky mistletoe ... dried snot ... impetigo ... marlpools ... coagulations of frogs ... smeared cat-mint on his palm ... [The men] brewed and pissed in splendour ... ' Like the boar, his snout is 'intimate with worms and leaves'. This is a richness that extends to desks, coins, pens, cars, 'boxes, | rags and old tyres' with a fascinated sense of sensuous detail apprehended with an immediacy prior to any ordering or investiture of meaning. It is the first draft of experience drawn out of memory. Such sensuousness recurs in *Tenebrae*. 'A Pre-Raphaelite Notebook', like its neighbour 'Terribilis Est Locus Iste', referring to Gauguin and the Pont-Aven school, presents a picture to match the almost lurid vividness of those painters,

> Primroses; salutations; the miry skull
> of a half-eaten ram; viscous wounds in earth
> opening.
>
> (*CP* p. 167)

The 'Earth's abundance' this poem speaks of is also in the preceding poem, the second of 'Two Chorale-Preludes' after Paul Celan:

> Silvery the black cherries hang,
> the plum-tree oozes through each cleft
> and horse-flies siphon the green dung,
> glued to the sweetness of their graft:
>
> immortal transience[.]
>
> (*CP* p. 166)

This version of 'great creating Nature', lies beneath everything. Its ooze is partly repellent but always compelling. It is 'the pierced slime' whose blind heat is nevertheless life, come to be crowned:

> The crocus armies from the dead
> rise up; the realm of love renews
> the battle it was born to lose,
> though for a time the snows have fled
>   ('Veni Coronaberis', *CP* p. 169)

There is a similar sense here to that of Whitman's 'libidinous prongs' ('Song of Myself', Chant 24) in these lines, and of the contradictions he struggled with of fecundity, procreation and sexual repression. Hill's poems present incessant flowering and fruition, but what is not resolved is whether this is part of the continuing rebirth of love or an empty and

meaningless organic reflex as in another poem of Celan's, 'Psalm', in
Michael Hamburger's translation:

> A nothing
> we were, are, shall
> remain, flowering[.][2]

Upon this profusion men seek to stamp, or to tease from it, mean-
ings that will render it into a bearable order. This seeking is the perpet-
ual voyage to that 'very ancient land indeed; / Aiaia formerly or Cythera
... / ... / ... by ageing poets sought ...' of the Sidney Keyes poem 'Sour
Land'[3] that Hill used as epigraph to the 1978 edition of *Tenebrae,* or
from the opening of the first 'Chorale-Prelude':

> There is a land called Lost
> at peace inside our heads.
> (*CP* p. 165)

Hill feels we are bound by that perpetual paradox of love renewing 'the
battle it was born to lose'. But it is a battle that must be waged for the
alternative is death, not just the death that will come, but the corollary
that acceptance of death entails indifference to life and pain, particularly
the pain of others. The world may be contemptible but it can never be
contemned for all its writhings. This is what Harold Bloom[4] calls Hill's
'desperate humanism', a racked but resilient sinew drawn taut by every
qualification and doubt. In *Tenebrae* it appears with least equivocation in
the poem '"Christmas Trees"' in praise of the German pastor and oppo-
nent of Hitler Dietrich Bonhoeffer. I quote the whole poem.

> Bonhoeffer in his skylit cell
> bleached by the flares' candescent fall,
> pacing out his own citadel,
>
> restores the broken themes of praise,
> encourages our borrowed days,
> by logic of his sacrifice.
>
> Against wild reasons of the state
> his words are quiet but not too quiet.
> We hear too late or not too late.
> (*CP* p. 171)

The delicate variations on the steady tetrameter (for example the successive
stresses on **'wild rea**sons') culminate in the poem's penultimate line. As he
arrives at that soft affirmation, made in such a common phrase, Hill shifts
the rhythm decisively from the regular stress and syllable pattern. It is not

a dramatic rupture, but the mildest of caesurae and a change which takes the poem out of its *elegiac* frame and puts its implications to the reader. We can no longer reside in a sorrowing identity with Bonhoeffer the victim but are given our own situation and responsibilities. It is these particular words that do this, registering the poem's meaning in the pitch of that rhythm.[5] It is a composure of the voice that Hill has Campanella speak of in 'Men Are a Mockery of Angels' (*King Log*, *CP* p. 78), another poem where the rhythms mime the meaning, and in a moment of resolution.

But such resolution is if anything even less frequent in *Tenebrae* than in Hill's previous books. A composure of the voice which is towards words that are 'quiet but not too quiet' is harder to come by than ever. The Word, that is said to make order out of chaos, retains, especially in poetry, its old faithless energies – 'The tongue's atrocities' ('History as Poetry', *King Log*, *CP* p. 84). Poetry, as a deliberate artifice, might be seen as a 'mesh of ornament', a 'labyrinth of abstract style' which locks life with its Midas touch – the 'stony vine' of *Mercian Hymns,* the 'sculpted vine' of 'Veni Coronaberis' – and turns everything to display. None of the meanings or 'truths' which might render this world orderly that are inspected in *Tenebrae* – not sexual love, or religion, which in any case fall upon each other, not England in its redolent and resonating nationhood, not the transcendence of the martyr – none of these can escape the debilitating *styles* of their expressions. The deep knowledge that the voice cannot be composed free of styles, in poetry free of the manners and traditions of the genre, has always been profoundly present in Hill's work. In seeking to compose itself, the voice must in some way contain the multitudes of those preceding voices in trying to gain its own 'directness'. For Hill this means turning a variety of predecessors to proper advantage, and in taking on the tradition in its own forms. In *Tenebrae*, as previously, these include the simplicity of the song and the very 'Englishe Eloquence' of the sonnet. But poetry in its artifice, with its possible poses and traductions, is but a concentrated mime of those elsewhere: in history, in 'life at large'.

'The realm of love', in its different but overlapping provinces, is the subject of the lyric sequence which opens *Tenebrae*, 'The Pentecost Castle'. The poems deal with the ancient entwinement of divine and sexual love. Each poem is an exclamation of love-longing or loss for a lover, or for Christ who is seen as a lover. Behind the poems stands the old Platonic conception which runs through the whole tradition of romantic love, that, in Owen Barfield's formulation in his *History in English Words*, 'love for a sensual and temporal object is capable of metamorphosis into love for the invisible and eternal'.[6] Hill has made use of a peculiar facet of this association in the lyrics of sixteenth-century

Counter-Reformation Spain where popular profane lyrics were re-written, or *parodied*, in religious terms by Lope de Vega and others. R. O. Jones,[7] one of Hill's source references, tells us that in this practice there was 'no barrier between the profane and the divine', and he quotes the anecdote Hill used as an epigraph for the publication of part of 'The Pentecost Castle' in *Agenda*:[8]

> ... San Juan de la Cruz sang, as he danced
> holding in his arms an image of the infant Jesus
> snatched from a crib, the words of an old love song:
> 'Si amores me han de matar / agora tienen lugar.'

Jones finds in this an 'ecstatic interfusion of the secular and divine', and there is a similar 'interfusion' of the sexual and religious in the 'Pentecost Castle':

> And you my spent heart's treasure
> my yet unspent desire
> measurer past all measure
> cold paradox of fire
>
> (8, *CP* p. 141)

Elsewhere in *History in English Words*, Owen Barfield argues that medieval English consciousness accrued 'a new element' of 'tenderness' in human relationships ('at any rate in the world of imagination') with the acceptance of such words from Latin through Early French as 'comfort', 'courtesy', 'grace', 'passion', 'tender', with secular rather than religious connotations.[9] This is evidence again of the interconnections within 'the realm of love'. But can we regard these transactions as unproblematic, smooth transitions without barriers? What we are considering here, as 'The Pentecost Castle' presents it, is not the bright ladder of Platonism with its rungs ascending from 'the loathly necklings' to the divine, but a complex turmoil that can be articulated through that continuing device of lovers, paradox:

> This love will see me dead
> he has the place in mind
> where I am free to die
> be true at last true love
>
> my love meet me half-way
> I bear no sword of fear
> where you dwell I
> dwell also says my lord

> dealing his five wounds
> so cunning and so true
> of love to rouse this death
> I die to sleep in love
> (9, *CP* p. 141)

This is 'Christ the deceiver' of the seventh song, the 'Crucified Lord', of the fourth 'Lachrimae' sonnet with his 'trim-plugged body, wreath of rakish thorn' (*CP* p. 148). The seductive complexities of the image of blood-sacrifice, its implicit sado-masochism, the sly calculation in that phrase 'dealing his five wounds', the eroticism that lies behind its offer of selfless love is all a part of the complex mythology that is Christ. The martyr's self-wounding that can, through obsessive self-regard, become self-seeking extends even to Christ, as I seek to argue in my accompanying essay on 'Lachrimae'. The second of the two epigraphs that preface the complete 'The Pentecost Castle' in *Tenebrae* is from Simone Weil and says:

> What we love in other human beings is the hoped-for satisfaction
> of our desire. We do not love their desire. If what we loved in them
> was their desire, then we should love them as ourself. (*CP* p. 137)

Following Weil then, 'I love you' does not mean what it says – ('taste of Pentecost's ashen feast'). Such words, such pain even, become but functions of our self-regard, the more admired for their elaboration:

> scrolled effigy of a cry
> our passion its display
>   (10)
> the night is so dark
> the way so short
> why do you not break
> o my heart
>   (11)
>
> as he is dying
> I shall live
> in grief desiring
> still to grieve
>
> as he is living
> I shall die
> sick of forgiving
> such honesty
>   (14)

In 'Lachrimae' Hill tussles with Pentecost's ambivalent gift of tongues in poems of utmost deliberation and literary complexity. 'The Pentecost

Castle', with its origins in music works similar matter through the simplest of lyric forms.[10] As it varies the theme through its spiralling series, it creates a beautiful translucent edifice, a castle in the air:

> how long until this longing
> end in unending song
>
> and soul for soul discover
> no strangeness to dissever
> and lover keep with lover
> a moment and for ever
>   (13)

Diversely, 'the land called lost', Cythera, that ideal land of love, is retraced to a very specifically English setting in the thirteen-sonnet sequence 'Apology for the Revival of Christian Architecture in England' (*CP* pp. 152–64). The sonnets affect an eloquent nostalgia for an England whose culture is almost organically at one with its largely comfortable, domesticated natural surroundings. It is a land of cultivated plants, the terrace-urn, laurel, the fir-grove; of furniture and the close preservations of cabinets and albums; of growth and dull velvety blooms:

>   Trees shine
> out from their leaves, rocks mildew to moss-green;
> the avenues are spread with brittle floods.
>
> Platonic England, house of solitudes,
> rests in its laurels and its injured stone,
> replete with complex fortunes that are gone,
> beset by dynasties of moods and clouds.
>
> It stands, as though at ease with its own world,
> the mannerly extortions, languid praise,
> all that devotion long since bought and sold[.]
>   (9 'The Laurel Axe')

Scattered in the portrayal of this England that 'grasps its tenantry', that in India unleashed 'the rutting cannon at the walls / of forts and palaces', are a whole series of lustrous set-piece rhythms and images, an eloquent ambiguous beauty which, in order to match its subject, comes consciously close to the overblown:

> where wild-eyed poppies raddle tawny farms
> and wild swans root in lily-clouded lakes.
>   (7)

> the children thread among old avenues
> of snowberries, clear-calling as they fade.
>   (8)
>
> In grange and cottage girls rise from their beds
>
> by candlelight and mend their ruined braids.
> Touched by the cry of the iconoclast,
> how the rose-window, blossoms with the sun!
>   (13)

How one is drawn to iconoclasm by the vision of this suppered gently decaying, and surviving England, yet also how potent are its mythological beauties. The residual dreams of a 'spiritual Platonic England' that informed the social criticism of Coleridge, Pugin and Disraeli, all of whom are invoked in the sequence's title and epigraphs, were always myths. But myths are real enough in a people's consciousness, and what Hill turns over, page by page, in this sequence is the affective ideology of a whole area of English mind and culture, and of its muddled dreaming.[11] It is not nostalgia but a profoundly sensed critique of nostalgia.

The word *tenebrae*, darkness, refers specifically to the darkness that falls upon the world at the crucifixion, and the offices of Holy Week that anticipate that darkness. It is also shadows, ghosts. *Tenebrae* closes with its title sequence, a group including two sonnets and some shorter poems of brief ferocity (*CP* pp. 172–4). The preoccupations of the book, particularly the tortuousness of desire – 'Our love is what we love to have' (4) – and the ecstasies of wounding and self-wounding, do not achieve a proportioned resolution. Rather their re-iteration is almost spat out with a punched clarity that even so cannot escape contradiction and self-contradiction:

> This is the ash-pit of the lily-fire,
> this is the questioning at the long tables,
> this is true marriage of the self-in-self,
> this is a raging solitude of desire,
> this is the chorus of obscene consent,
> this is a single voice of purest praise.
>   (6)

The 'this' I take to be the voice in darkness, the poem. As words it is the ash of purest inspiration; the interrogations of the worldly and of accusers; of solipsism and loneliness; of cheap acclamation. Finally, with uncommon, redemptive confidence, it is 'a single voice of purest praise', like that carefully composed for Bonhoeffer, 'quiet but not too quiet'.

The poem here is 'this' – impersonal. In the next poem, 7, there is a switch to the personality of the poet:

> He wounds with ecstasy. All
> the wounds are his own.

That huckster's reassurance takes us to the poet as entertainer, stripping his sleeve to show wounds and heart, cutting a caper with the word in his various guises: martyr, Lord of Misrule, Master of the Leaping Figures. Poetry is perpetually in self-regard: the self-regard of the poet as he exploits the word to his measure and the self-consciousness of the tradition. In this it is part of human intercourse – indeed a paradigm for it – with all its inherited expressions, all its styles and manners: 'The nominal the real'; 'the nothing that you say'. Perhaps however

> Music survives, composing her own sphere,
> Angel of Tones, Medusa, Queen of the Air,

but even this unworded purity of expression, taken as transcendence, offers a heartless perfection:

> and when we would accost her with real cries
> silver on silver thrills itself to ice.
>
> (8)

(This is similar to the passage on Averroes in 'Funeral Music 4' which also uses images of cold to suggest empty aestheticised perfection: 'an unpeopled region / Of ever new-fallen snow' (*CP* p. 73). It is hard to think of a work that challenges the terms of its own existence as remorselessly as *Tenebrae*. In doing so it 'thrills itself', and thrills its readers – but not to ice.

5 Things and words: *The Mystery of the Charity of Charles Péguy* (1983)

'Ah, les mots, mon vieux, les mots![1]

Take that for your example! But still mourn,
being so moved: éloge and elegy
so moving on the scene as if to cry
'in memory of those things these words were born.'

(10)

After the long, shifting account of Charles Péguy in Hill's poem, what are we to take from him? What sense is to be made, for what will he, who 'commends us to nothing', serve? The concluding moment of the poem is when we expect summary, a considered gesture, at least the ceremony of closure even though it might resemble stiffened custom and a bellowing 'with hoarse dignity into the wind'. Hill's tone, directed at his own contemplation as well as that of the reader, concedes little. 'Take that for example!' mingles defiance, the clean blow, with surly dismissal.

But take what? Take it how? Take Péguy and his end as an instance, a case to demonstrate some point? Or take him as exemplary, a model? There is no ready denouement. The stanza edges towards a close of the poem's complex meditation in an almost sidelong fashion, motivated or affected towards its 'cry', the sounds of 'éloge and elegy', eulogy and lament sliding the words against each other, the French word hinting at the danger of fulsomeness. The way these words work is entirely characteristic of the poem, and the eventual concluding 'cry', set as a quotation, retains the apparent guardedness of a phrase which is 'found' to be appropriate: ' "in memory of those things these words were born" '. But it is in fact a much more certain phrase, and one that embodies a central concern of the poem in its conjunction of ' "those things these words" '. The line asserts that these now living words bear upon 'things', have a bearing upon them. The poem relates to 'things', the world outside itself, specifically the life lived by Charles Péguy for which it is a work of celebration and sorrow, the genres of 'éloge and elegy'. None the less, although this is asserted, even yet the poem could be words into the

wind, carrying at best the euphony of 'éloge and elegy'. Hill's whole
poem travels over these two possibilities: circumstances in which the self-
sufficiency, the given facts of the world, events themselves, are moved by
words; and circumstances – poetry itself may well be among them –
where they seem without real object and yet are 'moving'. *The Mystery
of the Charity of Charles Péguy* is a poem about the potencies of words,
their direct issue, their distant weights and attractions, their formulations
of memories, images and ideologies, their sounds and resonances – about
what kinds of things can be done with words.

Phrasing that conjoins 'things' with 'words' echoes J. L. Austin's
book of lectures *How to Do Things With Words*[2] (hereafter *Words*), and
the implications of Austin's ideas are painstakingly taken up by Geoffrey
Hill in his essay 'Our Word Is Our Bond' (*LL* pp. 138–59). Austin's
interest is in the ramifications of what he calls 'performance utterance',
that is the use of words in which 'the issuing of the utterance is the per-
forming of an action – it is not normally thought of as just saying some-
thing' (*Words* pp. 6–7). For Austin the 'performative utterance' is an act,
and as such stands as a commitment in regard to the things to which the
words refer: 'Accuracy and morality alike are on the side of the plain
saying that *our world is our bond*' (*Words* p. 10). Thus, when *Péguy* begins
with the grim and nearly satiric evocation of the murder of Jean Jaurès
amid the bathos of his café supper, the event gives rise to speculation
about the part played in the assassination by Péguy's rhetorical attacks
upon Jaurès's pacifism. We have a clarification of the issues, a philoso-
pher's crisp identification of questions:

> Did Péguy kill Jaurès? Did he incite
> the assassin? Must men stand by what they write
> as by their camp-beds or their weaponry
> or shell-shocked comrades while they sag and cry?
>
> (1)

Did Péguy's utterance constitute, in Austin's terms, a 'perlocutionary
act', that is words which got someone to do something – as, for instance,
closing a door? But through this stanza the questions become less than
crisp as the verbs 'incite', and then especially 'stand by', reverberate with
their multiple associations. In plain saying does 'stand by' your words
mean: (1) be responsible for; (2) support, stick up for; (3) guard; (4)
await inspection; (5) be ready to shoot? The verb will cover the comic
military cliché 'stand by your beds!' and the support in desperate cir-
cumstances for 'shell-shocked comrades while they sag and cry'. It is not
easy to comprehend, plainly, what is being asked. And yet, this opening

section also shows the flowing of the blood that comes of what the poem later calls 'the metaphors of blood'. In metaphor, in the spoken and written word, the blood is painless as it spouts; but it can be made real, as by the archetypal political rhetoric of Shakespeare's Mark Antony who puts a tongue in each of the 'poor dumb mouths', the 'ruby lips', of Caesar's wounds and who saw how his trope, in the words of Hill's poem, 'spoke to the blood'. 'In Brutus' name' was there incitement or over-susceptibility to metaphor?[3] Yet in the whole of the suggested context here, such scrupulous worrying over 'performatives' might seem beside the point in that all these events, together with their characters and their intentions, are part of a grotesque and endlessly repetitive performance:

> History commands the stage wielding a toy gun,
> rehearsing another scene. It has raged so before,
> countless times; and will do, countless times more,
> in the guise of supreme clown, dire tragedian.
>
> (1)

The words perform, they are performed, and their performance is but part of history's theatre, put before us since Péguy's time, in the continuous performance of the cinematograph:

> The brisk celluloid clatters through the gate;
> the cortège of the century dances in the street;
> and over and over the jolly cartoon
> armies of France go reeling towards Verdun.
>
> (1)

Everything is representation.

Yet although Hill's Péguy, like Jaurès, and 'the cortège of the century', is caught behind glass, on view, still on guard, standing by, bull-headed, he is still defending his 'first position to the last word' as though there is some such thing as truth. (Péguy held to truth as an absolute, spoke of his projected *Cahiers* as *le journal vrai*, and emphasised this commitment by references to *le vraiment vrai*.) Here he is 'Truth's pedagogue', a naive idealist full of contradictions: 'raw veteran', 'Footslogger of genius, skirmisher with grace / and ill-luck', and so a proper figure for our scorn. The tone in this part of the poem is of wry mockery – even an indulgent patronising that extends to the cartoon armies of Péguy's fallen comrades, 'the old soldiers of old France' who 'crowd like good children wrapped in obedience', the *enfants* of a thousand stricken war-memorials. The wit and wordplay ('Dying, your whole life / fell into place') are distancing and self-protective: who would want to be implicated with such a man? He can also be accommodated by the conventional celebrations of tourism, represented to us through the guide's rote: "Sieurs 'dames, this is the wall / where he leaned and rested, this is the well / / from which he drank', and by statue, 'brave mediocre work / ... cornered in the park' (2). But across the grain of this mockery stand the words: 'still Péguy said that Hope is a little child' (1). Hill's line here is open, without any of the surrounding ironies. Its slightly awkward rhythm, close to plangency, and the somewhat pedantic inclusion of 'that', makes the line near a rather simple-minded affirmation, an effort to keep faith. The allusion is to Péguy's *Mystère: Le Proche du Mystère de la Deuxième Vertue*:

> Faith and Charity are going somewhere,
>   going purposefully,
> But Hope is like a child, who is not
>   interested in getting to its destination,
>   but is interested in the way itself.[4]

We have 'History' in command of the world, of such 'things' as are shown. But here we have the voice that strives to stay aside from the performance, that is without destination, that can do nothing, and yet is – 'embattled hope'. If we are seduced towards any of those accommodations, then Péguy now mocks us.

Resisting the given word requires a vision of something else. In the third section of the poem Hill evokes the lineaments of Péguy's vision, in which this 'Joseph' provides a dream of old France, rural, peaceable, simply religious, living in a steady round of physical and mental labour mutually respected, and, like Joan of Arc (whose spirit suffuses the whole) militant yet not militarist. The strength of Hill's account lies in his suggesting exactly those kinds of details and images that go to make up an indistinct and yet powerful consciousness of attachment and ideal:

> Yours is their dream of France, militant-pastoral:
> musky red gillyvors, the wicker bark
> of clematis braided across old brick
> and the slow chain that cranks into the well
>
> morning and evening.
>
>   (3)

Here Hill is colouring a vision of the 'matter' of France in a similar way to the lustrous images of his portrait of 'Platonic old England' in 'An Apology for the Revival of Christian Architecture in England' in *Tenebrae*:

> Trees shine
> out from their leaves, rocks mildew to moss-green;
> the avenues are spread with brittle floods[.]
>
> (*CP* p. 160)

Such images are the real nuclei of the attachments upon which any more conscious articulation of history depends. The lines from *Péguy* continue into such a history:

> It is Domrémy
> restored; the mystic strategy of Foch
> and Bergson with its time-scent, dour panache
> deserving of martyrdom.
>
> (3)

Hill's lines here cut deeper into a complex of notions in which Joan of Arc's native ground blends with the 'militant-pastoral' army of 1914. In achieving this, they perform the very process of memory Bergson describes: 'we feel vaguely that our past remains present to us'; 'a persistence of the past in the present'.[5] Within this animation, in the 'mystic strategy of Foch / and Bergson', two configurations of *élan* are conjoined: that positive quality of attack, of the spirited seizure of the initiative that obsessed French military theory at the start of the Great War in reaction to their supine humiliation of 1870; and Bergson's life principle of *l'élan vital*, the vital and original, impetus, which he opposed to mechanistic and determinist theories of life and evolution. In this phrase Hill catches the ironies of this complex exactly, playing the supposed, on-the-ground actualities of 'strategy' against the other-worldly connotations of 'mystic'. Indeed, by all accounts, the very particulars of Péguy's death, leading his section across a field towards the enemy, upright in a hail of bullets, exhorting the advance, must make him appear the embodiment of such a spirit, at once heroic and quixotic.[6] The contradictions of this moment are returned to time and again in the poem – Péguy, like his men, 'covered in glory and the blood of beetroots' (2). In one sense it is for 'musky red gillyvors, the wicker bark / of clematis braided across old brick' that Péguy dies.

Yet potent as it is, *real* as it is, the vision is always seen as a fable. This is explicitly stated, but the irony is carried in other ways too. There is a courtyard, 'crimped hedges', pigeons:

> and sunlight pierces the heart-
>
> shaped shutter-patterns in the afternoon,
> shadows of fleurs-de-lys on the stone floors.
>
> (3)

That tongue-in-cheek enjambment across stanzas teases the reader by
leading first into sentiment – the affect of the scene – before removing
into mere physical description. Also, while the whole poem makes use of
French words, phrases and loan-words, their presence in section 3 which
presents the first version of Péguy's vision, is particularly richly apparent:
archive, domaine, discourse, echelon, cadre, panache, in addition to the
evocative place-names. In English a liberal use of French words and loan-
words flourishes the diction, poses it in a particular way that makes us
sense the striking of an attitude. The doubts about the substance of this
fable are carried partly in these verbal effects, and, as they accrue, come
to face with *le vraiment vrai:* 'is this not true? Truly, if you are wise, /
deny such wisdom' (3).

The immediate, insistent truth is that of 'this world', the lean kine
of Joseph's dream, the world long ago taken by 'the lords of limit and of
contumely'. And it is in this world that Péguy lives, amid the labours and
acerbities of controversy: Dreyfus, the 'unsold *Cahiers* built like barri-
cades', the attack on Jaurès, the desperate farce of the murder. Giving
himself to the given, this world of street battles, proof-reading, and the
tying of parcels, Péguy seeks to redeem it, to transcend it. His entangle-
ment in the whole rhetoric of Jaurès's assassination, however, shows how
difficult such transcendence is. Instead it seems it is only mortal pride
that he achieves, and the appropriate bathos of his end recurs, this time
across a yet more drawn-out enjambment:

> So, you have risen
> above all that and fallen flat on your face
>
> 5
> among the beetroots ...

The way in which that phrase straddles the two sections mimes the way
in which the different responses to Péguy and his attitudes and circum-
stances persistently overlap and flow into one another. No sooner is one
perspective established than it dissolves, and the qualification and the
strength of an opposing view come into focus. This is the process of this
fifth, middle and longest section of the poem, which returns far less iron-
ically, to Péguy's vision, of 'old France', but yet sees its qualities and pos-
sibilities constrained and corrupted. Again, but this time with greater
gravity, the meanings impressed by the images of his ideal homeland are
traced out in all their deeply sensuous power. Its 'landscape and inner
domain' are joined – the outer and the inner, the real, the earth, the con-
ditioned, with the deepest imaginings of the ideal: grace, the unbur-
dened, the free. It is the process of the mind that can achieve this

transfiguration, 'the working / of the radical soul'. In this phrase, once more, is the remarkable and characteristic clustering of meaning, with the unelevated noun-principal denoting straightforward regular activity and labour, and the adjective and noun 'radical', and 'soul', going in apparently different directions, the one downwards to the root (as the succeeding stanzas confirm) though also with political, indeed icono-clastic, connotations, and the other upwards towards the ethereal, the heavenly. 'Radical' anchors 'soul', 'soul' irradiates 'radical', and its 'work-ing' connects with a whole series of opposites: the 'sun showers', hedgers and ditchers become seraphim, 'in a bleak visionary instant' become the 'winged ogives' with the 'criss-cross trodden ground'. The potency of landscape working through that 'radical soul – instinct, intelligence, / memory, call it what you will', is that it can be internalised. This works subliminally, at a barely perceived level of consciousness where images and associations form indissoluble significance. Here not only is this potency acknowledged, but its sensuousness suffuses the lines:

> Landscape is like revelation; it is both
> singular crystal and the remotest things.
> Cloud-shadows of seasons revisit the earth,
> odourless myrrh borne by the wandering kings.
>
>   (5)

The deep investiture of feeling and thought in place, in the earth, and the composure that might come of it, derives by specific allusion from the passage in Péguy's own long poem *Ève*. Its eighteen stanzas have the refrain 'Heureux ceux qui sont morts ... ', the first of them beginning:

> –Heureux ceux qui sont morts pour la terre charnelle,
> Mais pourvu que ce fût dans une juste guerre.[7]

The phrase will be echoed again in French, but here Hill writes, 'after' these lines:

> Happy are they who, under the gaze of God,
> die for the 'terre charnelle', marry her blood
> to theirs, and, in strange Christian hope, go down
> into the darkness of resurrection[.]
>
>   (5)

The dictionary gives the meanings of *charnelle* as 'carnal, fleshy ... sen-sual'.[8] Earlier, in section 2, the sensuality was displaced into the cheaply diminished 'sun-tanned earth'. But here the word emphasises a physical-ity to the attraction – 'marry her blood / to theirs' – that is consummated in burial, the word in English evoking of course 'charnel ground'. This 'investiture', however, does not entirely derive from Péguy's poem, but coincides with a concern previously evident in Hill's work, for instance in *Mercian Hymns*, IV:

> I was invested in mother-earth the crypt of roots
> and endings[.]

In fact, the whole working between place and history through 'instinct, intelligence, / memory', especially with its recognition of the vivid persistence of the child's memory, is common to both poems. The particular details of the country are known as they are in child's play; and, continuing, it is into this old intimate familiarity that the dead, 'in strange Christian hope, go down':

> into sap, ragwort, melancholy thistle,
> almondy meadowsweet, the freshet-brook
> rising and running through small wilds of oak,
> past the elder-tump that is the child's castle.
> $\qquad\qquad$ (5)

Poignantly, the child's tin soldier, and those 'scarred most scared', put us in mind of the adult legions lost among the haystacks and streams of this same landscape. But it is now an old country, worn and antique, preserved but bygone, and its sorrows quiver with an erect but hopeless dignity:

> $\qquad\qquad$ ... proud tears,
> proud tears, for the forlorn hope, the guerdon
> of Sedan, 'oh les braves gens!', English Gordon
> stepping down sedately into the spears.
> $\qquad\qquad$ (5)

The rhyming of 'guerdon'/'Gordon', and the wordplay 'Sedan'/ (Sudan)/'sedately', echoes one defeat with another, and, without seizing upon satire, none the less signals a withdrawal from that world whose elegy has just been so beautifully and sympathetically made. Swiftly then the myths of this same world are dissolved as the aura of Péguy's idealisations gives away to a sketch more familiar from another version of *la France profonde*, that of Zola's *La Terre*, a world of

> familial debts and dreads,
> keepers of old scores, the kindly ones
> telling their beady sous ...
> $\qquad\qquad$ (5)

For all its magnetism, Péguy remains crucially alienated from this myth-world and its religion, and looks from 'its truth and justice, to a kind of

truth, / a justice hard to justify'. Truth, justice, the ideal over-riding
absolutes that Péguy' saw at stake in the Dreyfus affair, and that he
sought to manifest and further in all his labours as writer, printer, proof-
reader and salesman of the *Cahiers*: these words play before our eyes,
echoing back to the 'juste guerre', and beyond to the ideal goal of
Péguy's work, and of his poem, which must itself be 'le mot juste'.[9] The
sixth section takes up the word immediately:

> To dispense, with justice; or, to dispense
> with justice. Thus the catholic god of France,
> with honours all even, honours all, even
> the damned in the brazen Invalides of Heaven.

How to do things with words! The simple dispensing with that first
comma effects the instant transition by which the ideal of Péguy's nation
becomes part of the reactionary ideology embodied in the persecutors of
Dreyfus. The 'labourers cap in hand' stand now before 'the catholic god
of France'. The play with words here is at its most sardonically intense,
a grim exchange of meaning, neat about-turns, whereby things are
brought round to the sanguine convenience of those 'lords of limit and
of contumely'. But the wordplay here is only part of the entire fabric of
the poem. If words are to be regarded as action, as 'bonds', and not as
'just saying something', then the clarity of what is said, Austin's 'plain
saying', is obviously of vast importance.

In his discussion of Austin in 'Our Word Is Our Bond', Hill even-
tually subscribes to the philosopher's principle of commitment to the
words one utters. But he finds Austin worryingly complacent about the
complexities that surround the achievement of 'accuracy' and 'plain
saying', and too confident of his capacity for transparent exposition.
Hill's effort, in his essay, is to direct attention to that complexity and
recalcitrance, and its inevitable implications for language. So,

> the very idea of a 'transparent' verbal medium is itself an inherited
> and inherent opacity. Where there is 'semantic content' it is most
> likely that there will be semantic 'refraction', 'infection' of various
> kinds. (*LL* p. 139)

Hill quotes Coleridge: 'our chains rattle, even while we are complaining
of them' (*LL* p. 142). Thus, the aphoristic flourish with which Austin
concludes one part of his argument, '*our word is our bond*', is itself capa-
ble of varying ambiguity: 'bond' as 'reciprocity, covenant, fiduciary
symbol', and also as 'shackle, arbitrary constraint, closure of possibility'
(*LL* p. 151). Hill writes:

> 'Our word is our bond' is an exemplary premiss, but if we take it in the positivist sense alone we take only part of its mass and weight. 'Our chains rattle ...' is the inescapable corollary for any writer who takes up Austin's stringent sentiment. (*LL* p. 143)

So the radical working with words, their 'mass and weight', 'refractions' and 'infections', demands the most fundamental senses of constraint and freedom, necessity and possibility, finality and hope. The *wordplay* which is so basic to Hill's method acknowledges the forces of each side of these dichotomies.

Ambiguity is the flexing of the determinations of language. Its play, as we seek to use and deploy it, demonstrates the frustrations of our own interventions towards meaning. In this respect, the word binds: ambiguity is the function of 'shackle, arbitrary constraint, closure of possibility'. Literary language might be seen as being able to turn this, together with other kinds of the common features among words, to advantage, since within its fictions it can exercise what Roland Barthes calls 'creative transgression', with the play among words delighted in as 'defections from the semantic system'.[10] This might give us the pleasurable nihilism of a Feste, his lady's 'corrupter of words', as he tries to confuse Viola:

FESTE: Why, sir her name's a word, and to dally with that word might make my sister wanton. But, indeed, words are very rascals since bonds disgraced them.

VIOLA: Thy reason, man?

FESTE: Troth, sir, I can yield you none without words; and words are grown so false, I am loath to prove reason with them.

(Act III, Scene 1)

Such a view of literature, if not of language at large, as cheerfully divorcing words from any bond or troth, might well have appealed to J. L. Austin, who, in a manner somewhat by-the-by, lights upon poetry for instances of where performatives need not 'be taken "seriously" ... I must not be joking, for example, nor writing a poem' (*Words* p. 9). Austin would presumably not have wished to deprive the poet and his reader of their *jouissance*, but would in turn expect them to acknowledge his argument that 'a performative utterance will, for example, be *in a peculiar way* hollow or void if said by an actor on the stage, or if introduced in a poem, or spoken in soliloquy' (*Words* p. 22). Accepting this, and so the playful fictionality of his utterance, offers a certain liberation to the author of the kind Hill associates with Sir Philip Sidney's dictum that 'the *Poet* he nothing affirmeth, and therefore never lieth'. Further, by 'faining notable images of vertues, vices, or what els', the poet, Hill suggests sarcastically, is 'generously propositioned'.

If he will accept that his art is a miniature emblem or analogy of res
publica rather than a bit of real matter lodged in the body politic
there is much scope for the exercise of serious and refined example.
(*LL* p. 143)

However, if obsession with ambiguity and the play between words,
and between words and things, might lead in these ways to an acknowl-
edgement of how we are conditioned, it can also, as Hill's essay and this
poem show, lead to other possibilities, difficult though these may be. The
sounding of words and their reverberations, from the constant reminder
of their contiguities as presented by the half-rhymes and rhymes of *Péguy*
to their multiple ambiguities ('must men stand by what they write') pre-
sents opportunities for suggestive connection. This is effected not by
what Jonathan Culler calls 'an unseemly rush from word to world',[11] but
by exploring the ways in which, as John Crowe Ransom puts it, 'the den-
sity or connotativeness of poetic language reflects the world's density'
(*LL* p. 151).[12] This exploration seeks to delineate relations between word
and world, and to sense and revel in the immanence of sentiments and
ideas through words. This 'fathoming of words as "heavy bodies"' (*LL*
p. 151; Hill is speaking of, and using, Hopkins's phrase here) does not
become merely the juggling of nuances, or, in Paul Ricoeur's term, 'a
case of vagueness'; rather is it a polysemic understanding which consti-
tutes, as Ricoeur says, 'the outline of an order, and for that very reason,
a counter-measure to imprecision'.[13] It will provide 'a kind of truth, / a
justice hard to justify'.

Concluding even part of an argument – inevitably not without some
rhetoric – and so setting oneself within some 'kind of truth', immedi-
ately opens up a different kind of problem. In *Péguy*, Dreyfus's judges
dispense 'a justice hard to justify'; indeed, they dispense with justice alto-
gether: '"A mort le Juif!"' Regarding this we have every reason for indig-
nation, and then an articulate human despair, and then a sense of moral
redemption that becomes however ultimately superior and self-regard-
ing. Righteousness, alienation, even martyrdom, bring here, as in Hill's
'Lachrimae' sequence (*CP* pp. 145–51), their own improper rewards. A
coruscating denunciation of the hypocrisies and complacencies of moral
self-righteousness concludes:

> We are the occasional just men who sit
> in gaunt self-judgement on their self defeat,
> the élite hermits, secret orators
> of an old faith devoted to new wars.

(6)

The violence of virtue, 'the wrath of the peacemakers', the self-inflicted-wounded, 'ecstatic at such pain', make their contribution, and

> Once more the truth advances; and again
> the metaphors of blood begin to flow.

Faced with a figure such as Péguy, with his stubborn commitment to absolutes, his vulnerability and worldly defeat and self-defeat, we, who like to think of ourselves as at least occasionally just, are eager to bestow the cachet of heroism, even martyrdom. The idea of eventual, transcendent victory in the realm of 'higher things' consoles and provides meaning for his life. But this consolation is suspect, the righteousness of martyrs is exposed, and even Christ's salute is unlooked for. The remainder of the poem focuses principally upon the war, and so upon Péguy's death and the suffering of the soldiers at large. Daniel Halévy, in his biography of his colleague Péguy, wrote of the young soldiers of 1914 that 'they knew they were going to die. They consented to that, but not meaning that their death was some incident in a butcher's shop. They wanted it to be a sacrifice illuminated by a certainty.'[14] The line from Péguy's *Ève* offers such a certainty, and 'we still dutifully read "heureux ceux qui sont les morts"'. But the tone now is more sceptical. Bergson developed a theory of 'duration', a qualitative concept of process, of evolution, that he saw as denying determination: '*we endure* and are therefore free'.[15] A less philosophical notion of what is to 'endure' is picked at through the specific word and its root in these lines from section 7:

> Drawn on the past
> these presences endure; they have not ceased
> to act, suffer, crouching into the hail
> like labourers of their own memorial
>
> or those who worship at its marble rote,
> their many names one name, the common 'dur'
> built into duration, the endurance of war;
> blind Vigil herself, helpless and obdurate.

The longing must be that something of them will prove durable in purpose or memory as, 'flesh into dust', their 'dreams of oblivion' replace paradise. The quest to attach meaning is yet more desperate through the eighth section, where the ironies of 'pour la patrie' are painfully evoked, though without ready satire. Rather there is a real regretful texture in the overblown pretensions of 'la France' to gather all her fallen children to the nation's 'august plenitude'. What can be held on to as 'the mind leaps / for its salvation' diminishes to a most abstract point of faith, barely

grasped: 'Whatever strikes and maims us it is not / fate, to our knowl-
edge.' Eventually, it comes down to the desperate ideal of self-abnega-
tion: 'Say "we / possess nothing; try to hold on to that"' (8).

As the soldiers' 'last thoughts tetter the furrows', a dreadful sim-
plicity and reduction appears through the poem. Thoughts aspirations,
love – 'mother, dad' – become a spattering across the pocked field. All
through the poem we have seen the mind at work in the world, in the
matter of ethics, language, ideology, attachments, visionary possibility.
In the final section of the poem, all those intricacies of living that Péguy
had fought over in his life and writing, and on which he finally turned
his back with the stoic, or ironic, acceptance of the barest choice –
'"Rather the Marne than the *Cahiers*"' – all these reduce to the simple
distinction between life and death:

> At Villeroy the copybook lines of men
> rise up and are erased. Péguy's cropped skull
> dribbles its ichor, its poor thimbleful,
> a simple lesion of the complex brain.
>
> (10)

And what is this human substance? *Ichor:* (1) the ethereal fluid, not
blood, supposed to flow in the veins of the gods; (2) (in transferred and
figurative use) blood; a fluid likened to the blood of animals; (3) (in
pathology) a watery, acrid discharge from certain wounds and sores
(*OED*). This contradictory matter of the self soaks into the earth, and
what it truly is, what Péguy finally gives, 'having composed his great
work, his small body', is a mystery. In that involved sentence over this
and the succeeding three stanzas of section 10, Hill approaches the
meaning of Péguy's death. A sequence of adjectival clauses build
towards the centrally placed main clause, which is, after all that expec-
tation: 'he commends us to nothing'. Péguy's testament, as the sen-
tence moves on from that point, is wordless, 'the body's prayer, / the
tribute of his true passion' for 'the Virgin of innumerable charities'.
However great that work is, or however slight a trickle into the soil, he
gives his all, whether in token of the Virgin's endless love of human
beings, or of the tinkling beady sous into countless collecting boxes. If
Péguy managed such a resignation then he leaves us no conviction of
apotheosis of any kind, no certain commendation. Deprived of such
ready meaning, the possibility hovers that 'moving' as they might be,
the words of the poem float in their own element, without connection
in the world of 'things': '"Encore plus douloureux et doux"', the actu-
alities of human pain rendered into the abstractions of 'affliction'.

Throughout the poem the density, self-awareness and sensuous richness of the language has anticipated this possibility and formed its own critique. What is exemplary is this proceeding engagement in language: if not the destination, then the 'the way itself'. This corresponds to the poem's portrait of Péguy, for he is exemplary in that he presents recalcitrant complexity, ambiguity, contradiction. The way is that of the foot-slogger, the pedagogue, the stubborn vigilant, doing his stint – no panache, no *élan*, but movement by inches. It is the complexity, ambiguity, contradiction of *things,* and of the *words* that would do things properly. Hill has done his Péguy justice: 'the ethical and the esthetic are one' (*LL* p. 150);[16] his great poem is 'a bit of real matter lodged in the body politic' (*LL* p. 143).

6 History as poetry: 'Churchill's Funeral' and 'De Jure Belli ac Pacis' (*Canaan*, 1996)

The epigraph Geoffrey Hill uses for the first poem in his sequence 'Churchill's Funeral' is from Edward Elgar's note on the 'Cockaigne' overture and contains the phrase 'knowing well the history'. It is apparent that Hill's poetry has always known history very well indeed. Historical figures and events have featured substantially from the beginning: 'Knowing the dead, and how some are disposed' ('Two Formal Elegies', *For the Unfallen*, 1959; *CP* pp. 30–1). Elegy, Requiem, 'In Memory', 'The Death of', 'Ode on the Loss of', 'Funeral Music' appear in titles of the earlier work to announce a compulsion towards commemoration of and respect for the past, and especially for the unfinished lives dismissed by the machinery of human history. Poems in *For the Unfallen* are notably appalled at the indifference of non-human nature: the tide that 'pastes / The sand with dead gulls, oranges, dead men' ('Wreaths', *CP* p. 41). It is in the face of such reduction, bound into the ferocious pun which concludes 'Requiem for the Plantagenet Kings' – 'and the sea / Across daubed rocks evacuates its dead' – that the poems seem meant to stand as memorials.

But equally that first volume is sceptical of the accomplishment of such memorial to a point that certainly unsettles the reader, and includes some remarkable instances of poems that turn mordantly upon themselves:

> Artistic men prod dead men from their stone:
> Some of us have heard the dead speak:
> The dead are my obsession this week
>
> But may be lifted away.
> ('Of Commerce and Society' 4, *CP* p. 49)

There is a discrepancy between all the customary furniture of monumental and poetic remembrance – 'our designed wreaths' and 'used words' ('Metamorphoses': 4 'Drake's Drum', *CP* p. 35), 'the laurels' / Washable leaves' ('After Cumae', *CP* p. 43) – and its subject which these poems measure. But even in that measuring, in recognising and satirising the self-importance of memorial – 'Here are statues / Darkened by laurel' ('A Pastoral', *CP* p. 54), the comic 'O near-human spouse and poet' ('Elegiac Stanzas on a Visit to Dove Cottage', *CP* p. 42) – the risk of falling into that discrepancy, or of being diverted by the poem's self-interest, is ineradicable. This awareness is most directly confronted in the elegy 'September Song' from *King Log* (1968), specifically with the parenthesis '(I have made / an elegy for myself it / is true)'. Here the ambivalence touching the poet's identification with the deported child, his near-contemporary, and the sense of his fashioning this poem for his own benefit, are set in a cadence that is at once tentative – a kind of aside – and deliberately mannered in the fractures of its free-verse enjambments. What is signalled here is made entirely explicit later in the volume in the title of 'History as Poetry' (*CP* p. 84). This sets forth the sense that the processes of poetry, its eloquence, its Pentecostal gift of tongues, transmutes the occurrences of history into poetry,

> Unearths from among the speechless dead
>
> Lazarus mystified, common man
> Of death.

The hubris of poetry, itself so often said to be enjoying a 'resurgence', is seen as lying in its presumption to bring the dead back to life, but deflated in the double meaning of 'mystified': Lazarus as bemused and Lazarus made mysterious. The poem ends with vicious sarcasm:

> The old
> Laurels wagging with the new: Selah!
> Thus laudable the trodden bone thus
> Unanswerable the knack of tongues.

It might seem from this severe reflexiveness that the pretence of poetry – or 'poetry' – is especially culpable in representing the dead for its own ends. This would be compounded by poetry's traditional claim to be the acme of our rhetoric, the most considered of utterances. But, in being so, it can be claimed that the genre is not uniquely self-interested but stands as representative of our speech at large. Since that speech is permanently susceptible the claim must imply more responsibility than satisfaction. The problems facing the poet in fashioning words that will fit – that are fit – are a model of those involved with language use within a wide variety of our discourses. A persistent image in Hill's prose work when discussing the exercise of language is of gravitational pull. For example in 'Our Word Is Our Bond' he quotes Hopkins's notion of words as 'heavy bodies' each with 'a centre of gravity' (*LL* pp. 151 and 194), and in 'Unhappy Circumstances' of 'the resistant inertia of "our stubborne language"' and 'the gravitational field of the *negotium*' (*EC* p. 16). And nowhere is this pull more apparent than in seeking words that might fill the discrepancy, words that might evoke the men and women who are misrepresented by the approximations and inflations of elegy and memorial. In 'History as Poetry' they are 'the speechless dead', yet more materially and harshly, 'the trodden bone'. The dead are the true matter of 'history', they are what matters, and Hill's attention to them is recurrently haunted by their very reduced materiality, often, in *For the Unfallen*, the sea's detritus, later,

> Péguy's cropped skull
> dribbles its ichor, its poor thimbleful,
> a simple lesion of the complex brain.

and the soldiers' 'last thoughts' that 'tetter the furrows' (*Péguy*, *CP* p. 193). By the intense insistence on these physical vestiges, this heartless reduction, Hill strives to evoke the unworded reality of 'the varied dead'. In the same way the processes of 'History' are evoked in a nearly inarticulate way that strives to evade rhetoric: 'Things happen' ('Ovid in the Third Reich', *CP* p. 61), 'Things marched' ('September Song', *CP* p. 67). The horror of these events and the loss of these lives, we must believe, have a reality outside our representations of them and outside the mythologies or 'histories' by which we make them meaningful. It is unbearable that we draw them to our own centredness but we do. Poetry has the self-regard to show this process at work. To make poetry out of historical 'subject-matter' is to reveal how 'poetic' the making of history out of the tetter of the past really is.

But in Hill's work there is no relaxation in this discovery. He registers but is not content to reside in the play of textualities. Persevering at Bacon's image of words as like a Tartar's bow which 'doe shoote backe vppon the vnderstanding of the wisest, and mightily entangle, and peruert the Iudgement', Hill allows himself ground to suggest that

> it is not inevitable that words rebel against all attempts at better distinction, even when rebellion and loss of distinction are the matter of their contemplation. ('The Tartar's Bow and the Bow of Ulysses', *EC* p. 31)

If it *were* inevitable then silence would be the only honourable course, so totally consuming would be the realisation of 'the tongue's atrocities'.

one dark day in the Guildhall: looking at the memorials of the city's
great past & knowing well the history of its unending charity, I seemed
to hear far away in the dim roof a theme, an echo of some noble melody

Elgar's words point to the way in which music, like poetry, can transmute
'history' into its own currency. The fancy is that the past offers its being
in the form of a musical theme, in the case of 'Cockaigne' one imbued
with an ideal national, specifically London, spirit. In a letter, Elgar wrote
of the work as 'cheerful and Londony, "stout and steaky"',[1] and Wilfrid
Mellers refers to the '*nobilmente* swagger' of Elgar's patriotic music.[2] Hill
concludes the first poem of 'Churchill's Funeral' (*Canaan* pp. 43–50)
thus:

> *nobilmente* it
> rises from silence,
> the grand tune, and goes
> something like this.

The 'tune' of Hill's sequence is far from 'grand' in the Elgarian sense and
the London it evokes is no cheerful land of Cockaigne. It is rather an
ironic counterpoint, another kind of knowledge from that Elgar 'seemed
to hear' in the Guildhall. It begins:

> Endless London
> mourns for that knowledge
> under the dim roofs
> of smoke-stained glass,
>
> the men hefting
> their accoutrements
> of webbed tin, many
> in bandages,
>
> with cigarettes,
> with scuffed hands aflare,
> as though exhaustion
> drew them to life[.]

Here 'the dim roofs' are those of the railway stations receiving exhausted
soldiers from the trenches or Dunkirk, and the entire sequence is ani-
mated by their figures, by the victims of the Blitz, and of the poor.
Epigraphs to poems III and V of the sequence are from William Blake,
and the whole work adopts and adapts something of his mode and sen-
sibility. The four-line stanzas echo the short lines in 'Songs of Innocence
and Experience', and III in particular, headed by these lines from *Milton*,
'*Los listens to the Cry of the Poor Man; his Cloud / Over London in volume*

terrific low bended in anger', carries also the ironic bitterness of 'The Human Abstract':

> The copper clouds
> are not of this light;
> Lambeth is no more
> the house of the lamb.
>
> The meek shall die rich
> would you believe:
> with such poverty
> lavished upon them[.]

The whole work is more 'London' than 'Londony', 'looking on Albion's City with many tears' (*Jerusalem* 31).

And the tears are due in part because the ideal notion of a city, a commonweal, has failed its people. They have made their sacrifices and kept faith and remained resolute in a pragmatic, practical way:

> fierce tea-making
>
> in time of war,
> courage and kindness
> as the marvel is
> the common weal
>
> that will always,
> simply as of right,
> keep faith, ignorant
> of right or fear[.]

'Fierce tea-making' comes as a perfectly judged bathos after the ideal abstraction that opens this poem with its evocation of 'res publica' – 'its whole shining / history discerned / through shining air'. It is a phrase too which compresses the 'Britain can take it' commonplaces of wartime propaganda, associates an instance of colloquial cliché ('as the saying is') with its warm circularity, and so tempts the reader with a flicker of condescending humour before mounting a forceful defence:

> who is to judge
> who can judge of this?
> Maestros of the world
> not you not them.

Their courage, kindness and tea-making should not be taken lightly by political or artistic 'maestros'. They are taken so however, and continue to be, for when the city that saw the 'blitzed / / firecrews' martyred (IV) comes to be rebuilt in the final poem, it 'reorders its own /

destruction, admits / the strutting lords / / to the temple'. Layering
associations by his images in a way that suggests the idea of a city's
archaeology revealed by the mutual processes of blitz and redevelop-
ment, Hill sets a picture of the 'brazed city' and its culture, specifically
its gutter press. The epigraph from *Jerusalem* to this poem is ' ... *every
minute particular, the jewels of Albion, running down / The kennels of the
streets & lanes as if they were abhorr'd*'. It concludes:

> Whose Jerusalem -
> at usance for its bones'
> redemption and last
> salvo of poppies?

By using the archaic word 'usance' in place of 'usury', Hill not only refers
to the city's traditional business (its 'usurous hand', says Blake in 'Holy
Thursday') but can include the second sense of 'usance': a period allowed
for payment. How long must the city wait? Ruskin is another antecedent
in the radically critical and ironic tradition to which this sequence
belongs. Poem II is prefaced by an epigraph from the Preface to *Unto
this Last* (1862), a work whose purposes Ruskin described as first to
define what wealth actually is, and second

> to show that the acquisition of wealth was finally possible only
> under certain moral conditions of society, of which quite the first
> was a belief in the existence and even, for practical purposes, in the
> attainability of honesty.[3]

However, an account of 'Churchill's Funeral' should not, I think,
content itself with emphasising the work's critical sense. It does level at
suffering and injustice and pick at the ideological matter of the nation,
but the poem is also suffused with a sense of the power of the 'grand
tune' of England. I have written of 'ironic counterpoint' and 'another
kind of knowledge', but the images realised here of the returned, nearly
childlike soldiers, 'strange homecoming / into sleep, blighties', (night-
ies), and the 'mangled voices / within the flame' of the Blitz, are
immensely resonant, affecting, nearly ceremonious. The reader is capti-
vated and drawn into them. For an English reader especially they have
the kind of potent associations perhaps felt more in the manner of 'a
theme, an echo of some noble melody'. It is itself 'image-making'. The
particulars of Churchill's funeral are nowhere directly mentioned in the
poem, but ceremony and procession, specifically in London, are part of
its warp. The chroniclers of Churchill's obsequies dwell on redolent place
names to indicate the route of the procession.

> From Westminster Hall, the coffin draped in the Union Jack and
> resting on a gun carriage, was drawn by sailors from the service he
> had led in two world wars, the length of Whitehall, the Strand, Fleet
> Street, and up Ludgate Hill to the entrance of St Paul's Cathedral,
> the pavements tightly packed with citizens all the way, every flag at
> half-mast ...
>
> The steam locomotive was the 'Winston Churchill' of the
> 'Battle of Britain' class, and the television picture of it from the air,
> streaming smoke as it cut its way through the winter English coun-
> tryside was for many the most memorable sight of a day rich in cer-
> emony and solemn mass movement.[4]

The traditional stage-management of such ceremonies in English life,
especially the journeying procession, is impressed deeply into the national
consciousness. Blake's mapping of London in *Jerusalem*, and his preoccu-
pation with the orphans' procession of 'Holy Thursday', is a counterpart
to this: 'Los ... walk'd difficult. / He came down from Highgate thro'
Hackney & Holloway towards London ...' (31). Although Blake is of
course routinely co-opted by national enthusiasm in the simple reference
'Jerusalem', his vision was mightily different:

> So spoke Los, travelling thro' darkness & horrid solitude;
> And he beheld Jerusalem in Westminster & Marylebone
> Among the ruins of the Temple,

The manner of both litanies is echoed in the list of blitzed churches Hill
sets as epigraph to IV: '*St Mary Abchurch, St Mary Aldermanbury, St
Mary-le-Bow* ...'. There are two sensibilities at work, even at war with
each other in 'Churchill's Funeral'. One is sceptical, ironic, critical, the
other feels and represents the feeling of belonging, in part sentimental,
also tragic. No people can live successfully without a sense of belonging,
what Ruskin called 'social affections'. It is the task of the civic nation, the
res publica, to surround that integument with justice and security. But its
lineaments can also be made into a distracting fantasy making possible
evasion of the question 'Whose Jerusalem?' The answer must be the
Jerusalem of us all, for in the end it is all our funerals.

Writing in '"Envoi 1919"' of the techniques of 'modernist' poetry, specif-
ically of Pound's 'Hugh Selwyn Mauberley', Hill notes its use of 'rapid jux-
tapositions and violent lacunae ... phrase callously jostling with phrase,
implication merging into implication ... sententiae curtly abandoned' (*EC*
pp. 94–5). This describes of course those aspects of Hill's style that he has
developed from that source, a feature of his work so fascinatingly and dis-
ruptively offset by the contrasting capacity for strophic passages of

extended eloquence and lyrical plenitude. In his work at large, and some-
times within individual poems, each mode seems to criticise the other.

The eight poems of the sequence 'De Jure Belli ac Pacis' (*Canaan*
pp. 30–7) contains both elements, and their 'jostling' is the necessary
stylistic embodiment of the struggle inherent in the work's subject.
'History', I am arguing, is recurrently represented as 'poetry' – images
and cadences of a lyrical power often akin to the working of music –
although this 'poeticising' is not confined to the literary genre of verse
but is ubiquitous in our representations of the past. Thus our history and
present time can seem a collage relieved of reasoning connection. In 'De
Jure Belli ac Pacis' we encounter a familiar set of references that can be
collocated under the heading 'Europe': resistance, Maastricht, cities in
flames, 'Schiller's chant', 'this common Europe', holocaust, Schindler. A
telos or 'History' for 'Europa' in the twentieth century could readily be
drawn up which would include these components, make much use of the
word 'community' and climax with 'Ode to Joy' as a football anthem.
But the parts are rarely made to cohere, and that *telos* is in any case an
understandably anxious one, built literally out of ruins and fearful of the
future. Sadly they have become part of the jostle of the day.

Hill's title, kept in its magisterial Latin, speaks for a transcendence
of this anxiety and conflict. 'The Laws of War and Peace' no less: an over-
arching order, a codification and means of resolution. Grotius
(1583–1645), himself a political refugee, sought to provide in his *De Jure
Belli ac Pacis* a table by which conflict could be resolved and justice done
on a universal scale. His was a modern ambition, rational governance by
charter, the rule of law among nations. But the strife of his own day,
specifically the Thirty Years War, and the subsequent history of Europe,
specifically of the Second World War with which this poem is concerned,
sets Grotius's project upon a lonely pediment of irony. The 'Europa' con-
catenation seems plangent wishfulness, elbowing for some space against
perpetually incipient opportunism and barbarity.

But there is another striving in Hill's 'De Jure …' which is its own
attempt to assemble at least some juxtaposition that will make sense and
comprise a comprehensible history. The mode of the poems, combining
'phrase callously jostling with phrase, implication merging into implica-
tion … sententiae curtly abandoned' with passages of discursive asser-
tion, enacts the struggle to make a meaning of value from what there is
of the past: 'letters, codes, prayers, / film-scraps, dossiers, shale of
crunched shellac' ('De Jure …' VIII).

One feature of Hill's own tesselation is to borrow the classic histor-
ical mode of the exemplar. The poems' dedicatee, Hans-Bernd von

Haeften (1905–44), Christian lawyer and diplomat, was part of the
'Kreisau Circle', the clandestine opposition to Hitler which both worked
towards his overthrow and sought to establish detailed plans for German
renewal after Nazism. He is not an obvious hero. Of those involved in
the July 1944 plot to assassinate Hitler, the Archangel Michael, whom
von Haeften saw as the 'angel of German history' fighting the dragon,
'unseeing, unbowed' (II), might be better represented by the maimed
warrior Von Stauffenberg. Von Haeften was a bureaucrat and not at all
minded towards martyrdom.

The second poem in the sequence focuses upon the externals of von
Haeften's death with the same kind of harsh, insistent materiality, 'here
… here', I have noted elsewhere:

> Glare-eyed, you spun. The hooks are still in the beam;
> a sun-patch drains to nothing; here the chocked
> blade sluiced into place, here the abused blood
>   set its own wreaths.

But, for all Von Haeften's comparative obscurity, the modern jostle
reaches too far for the poet to have him to himself for contemplation.
Poem IV begins:

> In Plötzensee where you were hanged
>   they now hang
> tokens of reparation and in good faith
> compound with Cicero's maxims, Schiller's chant,
> your silenced verities.
>   To the high-minded
> base-metal forgers of this common Europe,
> community of parody, you stand ec-
> centric as a prophet.

Legationsrat von Haeften, who twenty years later might imaginably have
worked in the European Commission, has had his credentials accepted.
The pendant half-line, 'hanged / they now hang' mimics the clumsy
embarrassment often attendant on official wreath-laying, a shadow of
irony crosses the earnest allowance 'in good faith', and the emptiness of
'verities' registers the manageable reduction of von Haeften's words and
fate. Yet of course officialdom cannot be entirely derided, for the poet
has after all made the same hero for himself, 'it is true': 'There is no better
/ vision that I can summon:'. But the colon at the end of that phrase
takes that acknowledgement forwards, and into an idea which, in the
context of the discourse of contemporary polity, is truly eccentric.

> There is no better
> vision that I can summon: you were upheld
> on the strong wings of the Psalms before you died.
> Evil is not good's absence but gravity's
> everlasting bedrock and its fatal chains
> inert, violent, the suffrage of our days.

In court, Von Haeften was asked how he could have conspired against Hitler. 'Because,' he replied, 'I consider the Fuhrer the executor of the evil in history.'[5] Those last three lines of the poem also appear to relate to a passage of Von Haeften's writing pointed to in one of Hill's notes to the poem in its original publication in *Agenda*: [6]

> Hegel's comment on Napoleon, 'I have seen the world's reason (*Weltvernunft*) riding' is a repulsive reminder of how cheaply previous generations thought they could discover an immanent purpose at work in history. The only meaning that we can really discover is the lesson that is always fresh, namely that all human effort is vain, that all human arrogance is doomed and that all the roots of human independence are insubstantial.[7]

The eccentricity I believe lies in the uncompromising challenge to hopeful thought – the fixed optimism, for instance, that surrounds the concept of a 'common Europe'. Yet if these words represent Von Haeften's 'bedrock' belief, it was not a vision that led him to contemplative despair. On the contrary his was evidently a *vita activa*, albeit of a grindingly unglamorous kind, and as a jurist and diplomat he is likely to have made particular contributions to the Kreisau project

> that Europe might become a community of pluralistic states prepared to settle conflicts in a rational spirit, instead of a collection of powers whose arbitrary moral standards could only lead to irresponsible action.[8]

'You foretold us', writes Hill in poem III.

> You foretold us, hazarding the proscribed tongue
> of piety and shame; plain righteousness
> committed with much else to Kreisau's bees
> for their particular keeping.

Hidden together in the beehive, layer on layer, are commitments of apparently different kinds, both of which were to lead to Von Haeften's committal: the grand, rising prescription – De Jure Belli ac Pacis – and the laden sense, always dragging downwards, of 'evil' as 'the suffrage of our

days'. Himself 'hazarding the proscribed tongue / of piety and shame',
Hill produces that marvellous cadence:

> Evil is not good's absence but gravity's
> everlasting bedrock and its fatal chains
> inert, violent, the suffrage of our days.

It carries its import, buffeted by clusters of stresses that seem like the
blows of its realisation, through a nearly continuous movement till it
halts at '/ inert, violent', before completing three iambs of an achingly
stoical determination. Momentarily, in this context, we think we are
about to read the word 'suffering', but 'suffrage' is grimmer, and, with
its senses of intercession, help and support, and consent, besides the
now primary political sense, massively more resonant. In such lines the
poem seeks to compose its own voice amid the throng of votaries and
appropriators. Clearly they stand apart from other 'tokens' as, in the
last analysis, the entire sequence must if it is not to be but part of the
general jostle: 'late / gold of Europa / in her brief modish rags – /
Schindler! Schindler!' (VII).

   But if the poem does recoil, and shows exactly what it is recoiling
from and why, what is the substance of its own attention to its subject?
If, as the sequence's opening poem suggests, Von Haeften is now used
like a public monument,

> your high-strung
> martyred resistance serves
> to consecrate the liberties of Maastricht?

the reader will seek to see what might be the proper manner and use
of saluting him. Is there, from the babble of histories, variously poet-
icised, a true story? Grotius's title stands like a sorrowful arch over the
poem, a mighty inscription that would will an eternal realm of justice
into being. But it is not the world as it is, nor, presently, does it appear
part of 'an immanent purpose at work in history'. The aspiration is
heroic and never to be abandoned, but it belongs in the realm of
'but if'.

> But if – but if; and if nowhere
>   but here
> archives for catacombs; letters, codes, prayers,
> film-scraps, dossiers, shale of crunched shellac,
> new depths of invention, children's
>   songs to mask torture ...
> Christus, it is not your stable: it will serve
> as well as any other den or shippen

the arraigned truth, the chorus with its gifts
of humiliation, incense and fumitory,
                                        Lucerna,
the soul-flame, as it has stood through such ages,
ebbing, and again, lambent, replenished,
                            in its stoup of clay.

This last poem of 'De Jure Belli ac Pacis' carries the epigraph '*Hinricht-ungsstätte war ein Schuppen im Gefängnis...*' ('The place of execution was a shed in the prison'). This shed becomes a den, as of wild beasts, and, implicating the reader by language shift, a shippen (*Schuppen*). We might have thought the word archaic but it is a byre or stable, although 'Christus, it is not your stable'. But it will serve as this poem serves, cautiously but boldly in the end, as an Adoration.

However it is not a traditional Adoration and we are led to ask more about what is represented by this journey to Von Haeften's place of execution and about the achievement and significance of such homage in the specific form of a poem. The focus of the respectful 'chorus' is 'the arraigned truth'. Here the allusion to the nativity suggests that the presentation of the Christ child already prefigures the trial of Christ: that 'the truth' is from the beginning subject to account, charge, interrogation. More particularly, as reading these poems keeps showing us, discerning 'the truth' among the contending rhetorics of 'history' is perpetually fraught, and in a poem no less than elsewhere as the 'interest' of its making makes its own claim. It might be argued that the poet should turn away altogether from such a subject knowing that proper commemoration is flawed and at worst exploitative. But the world at large does not deny itself such recollection. Memorials of every kind – monuments, museums, the preservation of concentration camps, of the room in Plötzensee, films, television series, publications of every kind – proliferate. They answer a profound need to recollect. Hill's work shows that need, inflected by a sense of uneasy relief that might be common to those of his generation old enough for the Second World War to be a decisive presence and memory, but young enough, and fortunately enough placed, to have escaped its worst torments. 'Ovid in the Third Reich' and 'September Song' come to mind as dealing with this topic as does the consideration of St Thomas in 'Canticle for Good Friday': 'He, / As yet unsearched, unscratched, / / And suffered to remain / At such near distance' (*For the Unfallen, CP* p. 38). Most of us situated with the leisure to read poetry are at 'such near distance' and this realisation too draws our witness.

As for the nature of such a poem's achievement and significance, the implication must be that the words be regarded as a kind of action.

Although of course we act all the time in variously serious or desperate circumstances in working and personal life, most of us, 'unsearched, unscratched', do not know, and will be thankful never to have to know, how we might act in the high extremes of threat and conscious moral choice. Such experience as we have might not give us confidence. In 'De Jure Belli ac Pacis' the realm of action is especially at issue given the underlying fact of Von Haeften's eventual choice to assent to the risks of the assassination plot after spending his entire working life deep in the *negotium* of practical affairs, specifically the effort to create some conditions for the establishment and implementation of laws of war and peace. Laws are composed of words which, enacted, we hope will produce justice which we hope will be true, rather than a

> Smart whip-tap at boot-top, absolute
> > licence of the demons
> to wreak their correction[.]
>
> > > (VII)

But justice, an avatar of truth – hopefully the conjuring of truth – is equally difficult and continually arraigned. The philosopher Gillian Rose:

> If metaphysics is the *aporia*, the perception of the difficulty of the law, the difficult way, then ethics is the development of it, the *diaporia*, being at a loss yet exploring different routes, different ways towards the good enough justice, which recognises the intrinsic and the contingent limitations in its exercise.[9]

We will say 'good enough justice' can never be complacently accepted as good enough, and recognition of 'the intrinsic and the contingent limitations' must still include striving against them. But we will surely also acknowledge the realism of Rose's formulation, and thus that the effort to establish the law, (De Jure ...) will be in and therefore *through* words, 'at a loss yet exploring'. The poem may be a modest and obscure artifact, and may make 'nothing happen', but it is a model of this restless problem. It is a circle of attention, of deliberation – without extenuation – where, if the poet is up to the task, every detail of the weights, rhythms, contexts and histories of the words in which the poet's subject consist can be registered. The ethical demand upon the poem is to use the leisure of this attention to be part of the exploration Rose speaks of, and it is this that gives it the quality of an act. Nevertheless, memorial must seem, although the most compelled, still the most impotent of poetic acts: 'What shall the poet say, / what words inscribe upon your monument?' cries Hecuba in Euripides' *Trojan Women*. Discussing Hecuba's lament, Martha Nussbaum dwells upon the ethical importance of words in

such a relatively inactive case in order to indicate that proper
response, in speech, passion, and circumscribed action, can be just
as much a virtuous act as a big heroic deed. Narrowing the scope
for movement does not always remove the opportunity for excel-
lent perception. [10]

The narrowed scope of the poem is where the poet is most aware of the
limitations and contingencies of language, yet is also most free to nego-
tiate them.

> I imagine singing I imagine
>
> getting it right – the knowledge
> of sensuous intelligence
>   entering into the work –
> spontaneous happiness as it was once
> given our sleeping nature to awake by
>   and know
> innocence of first inscription
> ('That Man as a Rational Animal Desires the Knowledge
>   Which is his Perfection', *Canaan* p. 2)

7 *The Triumph of Love* (1998)

*Although salvation may not lie in literature, nevertheless, there is
and has been a way to salvation there for many.* (Petrarch)[1]

> Whose lives are hidden in God? Whose?
> Who can now tell what was taken, or where,
> or how, or whether it was received:
> how ditched, divested, clamped, sifted, over-
> laid, raked over, grassed over, spread around,
> rotted down with leafmould, accepted
> as civic concrete, reinforceable
> base cinderblocks:
> tipped into Danube, Rhine, Vistula, dredged up
> with the Baltic and the Pontic sludge[.]
>
> (XIII)

There are many themes in *The Triumph of Love* – those the poet 'has
buzzed, droned, / round a half-dozen topics (fewer surely?) / for
almost fifty years' – but in my reading the poem is dominated by Hill's
effort to grapple with, to honour and in some sense to do justice by
all these unlived and unliveable lives – 'the brute mass and detail of
the world' (LXX). Given the title, this effort might be expected to seek
to discover whether the meanings gathered around the term 'Love' can
be pitted against this world, is there a sense in which it could be said
to 'triumph'? If so it will not be of the manner Ben Jonson cultivates
in 'Her Triumph' from his sportive sequence 'A Celebration of Charis':
'See the chariot at hand here of Love / Wherein my lady rideth!' The
baleful cast of Hill's poem seems closer to Shelley, whose chariot in
'The Triumph of Life', like that of Hegel's History, rides over the
bodies of the slain, and is checked only by the image of Dante 'returned
to tell / / ... the wondrous story / How all things are transfigured
except Love'. There is no such 'wondrous story' readily available in
The Triumph of Love. Indeed the word 'love' rarely appears, and then
in a heavily defended context as though its very utterance is hard-won

like the gently comic but moving endearment of LVII: 'My dear and awkward love, we may not need / to burn the furniture'.

Consideration of the immediate source of Hill's title, Petrarch's *Trionfo d'Amore*, shows how Love itself might be seen as 'dear and awkward'. Petrarch's is an allegorical poem cast in the mode of a Roman procession in which triumphant Amore, in Morley's Tudor translation[2] 'this great myghtye king', is attended by her many famous captives such as Caesar, Phèdre, Menelaus and eventually Petrarch himself. For Petrarch Love is more Eros than Agape. It is the wickedly accurate Cupid whose darts inflict so much confusion and disaster upon gods and humans alike. This awkwardness includes the transfixing of Petrarch himself in his restless devotion to Laura, a devotion that is none the less dear to him. This tension is commonly figured in the oxymorons so characteristic of Petrarch's style, familiar through his English imitators Wyatt and Surrey, and instanced in such lines from Morley's rendering of the *Trionfo* as 'So of my love's beautye dyd I make / Myne owne death' (III, 151-2) or 'content to burne is my delight' (III, 204). It is a figure Hill employs in one of his mentions of love at the end of section XCVI of his *Triumph* when he writes of 'the hatred that is in the nature of love'. Beyond those elements of unlaced posturing in Tudor love poetry, these shadows of paradox point to a different concept of Love in the Petrarchan tradition, one that is suggested more by Petrarch's Latin title for his *Trionfo*: *Triumphis Cupidinis*. 'Cupidity' – 'inordinate longing or lust; covetousness ... Inordinate desire to appropriate wealth or possessions' (*OED*) – puts a wider construction upon 'Love', and indeed, in the whole sequence that constitutes Petrarch's *Trionfi*, Love, which fails to ensnare Laura, is vanquished by her in the person of Chastity, Chastity in turn is vanquished by Death, Death by Fame, Fame by Time and Time by Divinity. To no degree does Hill re-construct the confident allegorical progression of the *Trionfi* – his manner and technique is in fact far more reminiscent of the restless, questing, occasionally self-flagellating voice of the *Canzoniere*. But in his own *rime sparse* – 'scattered rhymes' as Petrarch called that other sequence – Hill does, in a vision of the world most compelled by that 'brute mass and detail', drive at each element in Petrarch's scheme, evoking the apparently incongruous *Vergine bella* of the *Canzoniere* both as emblem for supplication and the eternal witness of the rapine of death, fame, and time, and what might or might not be 'hidden in God'. It is a pursuit demanding and tortuous enough to require the deliberation, anticipation, allusiveness, and especially the doublings-back, characteristic of the strategies of classical rhetoric:

> *Ad te suspiramus,*
> *gementes, flentes*: which, being interpreted,
> commits and commends us to loving
> desperately, yet not with despair, not
> even in desperation.
>
> (CIX)

Here the wrought use of the rhetorical figures of paronomasia ('commits
... commends'), and polyptoton ('desperately ... despair ... desperation'),
the severe line-cuts and the relief of the qualifiers, 'yet not ... not / even', work
in tension to achieve a balance where 'loving' is challenged but not counter-
manded. Like 'the soul-flame ... in its stoup of clay' at the end of the sequence
'De Jure Belli ac Pacis' (*Canaan*, p. 37), such surviving assertions are the
poem's guarded triumphs. They are defiant, as in the culminating defence of
poetry itself near the very end of the poem, but never triumphalist.

The poem's representation of 'Life' in the Shelleyan sense, whilst
not cast as a Roman-style Triumph, has some recurrent elements of
masque, or more specifically 'kermesse', a 'kermesse of wrath' (CXXIV)
evoking the grotesquerie of Bruegel, Goya and more specifically the
gross caricature of Jacques Callot's clowns, 'hideously-festive-death's
foragers' (XXVIII). The phenomenon of *representation* is important in
the poem. The constant allusion to pictorial, literary and other references
makes us perpetually aware of mediation, of how 'Life' is made a specta-
cle for us, a 'carnival' where 'The slaughterers relish this work / of sport
... hoyda! / hoyda! – heel-kicking their nags'. This can include a
palimpsest in which the fiery furnace of the Book of Daniel is covered by
images of the Holocaust. Hill, by deployment of tone, shows how easily
these can be consumed with an air of connoisseurship:

> Permit me:
> refocus that Jew – yes there,
> that one. You see him burning,
> dropping feet first, in a composed manner,
> still in suspension,
> from the housetop.
> It will take him for ever
> caught at this instant
> of world-exposure.
>
> (XX)

As well as fixing the horror of the Warsaw ghetto, the call to the projec-
tionist recognises the aestheticised prurience that attends the contem-
plation and exploitation of its images:

> Schauspieler? –
> Run it through again and for ever
> he stretches his wings of flame
> upon instruction.

Hill's appalled contemplation of the Shoah is not, as his critic Adam Kirsch alleges, a 'condemnation of it louder and more sincere than everyone else's [treating it] as in some sense a personal affront'[3] but a consideration that includes a no less appalled understanding of how the arrangement and presentation of its images and documents can be sensationalist and morally complacent. That he, like all of us, has become an audience of 'the Holocaust', a voyeur even, is a fact Hill reminds us of time and again. The indissoluble alloy of information and spectacle provided by film and photography in the twentieth century is a long-standing preoccupation, appearing for instance at the outset of *The Mystery of the Charity of Charles Péguy*:

> The brisk celluloid clatters through the gate;
> the cortège of the century dances in the street;
> and over and over the jolly cartoon
> armies of France go reeling towards Verdun.
>
> (*CP* p. 183)

The obvious concomitant of this concern with the ways of representation is a recognition of the artifice of the poem and of all language, hence, in *The Triumph of Love*, the foregrounding of classical rhetoric, in particular the antithetical modes of *laus et vituperatio*, which serves to point up the device involved in all utterance. This is an inflection of the reflexive concern with language that has always been prominent among the 'half-dozen topics' of Hill's poetic career. It has always been based upon a historical sense, and upon a conviction 'that "utterance" and "act" are not distinct entities'. Hill immediately supports this contention by quoting the philosopher Rhush Rees: 'For we speak as others have spoken before us. And a sense of language is also a feeling for ways of living that have meant something.' ('Poetry as "Menace" and "Atonement"', *LL* p. 11) 'As others have spoken before us' and as others speak:

> I have introduced,
> it is true, *Laus et vituperatio*
> as a formality; still this formal thing
> is less clear *in situ*. That –
> possibly – is why I appeal to it. The Angels
> of Sacral Equivocation, they now tell me,

are redundant: we have lost the *Bloody Question*
[*vide* State Trials (Elizabethan) – ED].
Though you can count on there being some
bloody question or other, one does more
than barely survive. Less hangs on the outcome,
or by, or around, it. Why do I think –
urgently – of beach-sewage?

(CXLII)

The cross-cutting between different registers and verbal contexts in this passage is typical of the whole poem which is a concert, sometimes a cacophony, of different voices. The use of, and reference to, rhetoric is the most signal reminder that 'others have spoken before us', and how. Here the parodied stiffness of 'it is true' (which must echo 'September Song') is at once matched by the parody of contemporary, colloquial informality – 'this formal thing' – another interpolation by the ever more harassed and exasperated off-stage ED (Who he?), before Disgusted chimes in from the saloon bar ('there's always some bloody question or other …'). But questions demand answers, and the Tudor inquisitor's 'Bloody Question' was not badinage but an instance where 'utterance' and 'act' were truly joined, where rhetorical eloquence was seriously a 'life skill'. The passage continues by adducing Moltke, the Bonhoeffer brothers and Hans-Bernd von Haeften, martyrs of the opposition to Hitler who all suffered the Bloody Question. Throughout his work, Hill has been transfixed by the model of those who faced ultimate responsibility for their own words – Mandelstam, Southwell, Péguy – individuals for whom speech and act turned out to be far from distinct. To be transfixed however is not to assume their company. Hill honours them, here and elsewhere, says they 'did / nobly thereby', but he mimes a hesitancy, even a mannerism, in that line-break, and continues in the closure of the section to cut away the ground of his own tribute:

Late praise costs nothing.
To the Angels of Inconclusive Right
on Both Sides, to the Angel of the Last
Minutes, to the Angel of Our
Estimated Times of Arrival and Departure.

Wordplay, the whole panoply of rhetoric whether formal and deliberate or unconsciously reflexive, is not decorative or superfluous to the ground of what is being said, but ineluctably of that ground. To be casual about words is indictable, and responsibility bears heavily even upon the proof-reader:

> For wordly, read worldly; for in equity, inequity;
> for religious read religiose; for distinction
> detestation. Take accessible to mean
> acceptable, accommodating, openly servile.
> *Is that right, Missis, or is that right?* I don't
> care what I say, do I?
>
> (XL)

The discovery in the same poem of Bonhoeffer and Max Miller does not arrive as part of an empty eclecticism. The nexus is the Second World War, the event that bestrides the poem in elegy, in anger, as *exemplum* and as memory. Hill – born 1932 – shows the boy, whose world 'spraddles' a couple of West Midlands villages, listening to the wireless, reading *Radio Fun*, poring over his aircraft recognition cards, convincing himself of the respective capabilities of the Fairey Battle and Swordfish, seeing a warship in a water tower and the distant but awesome spectacle of the bombing of Coventry: 'huge silent whumphs / of flame-shadow bronzing the nocturnal / cloud-base of her now legendary dust' (VII). 'Whumph' comes straight from a comic strip and so the clause contains the sensibility of the child's experience ('mouth full of blood and toffee') at the confused frontier of the real and imaginary, and the retrospective awareness of how the Blitz has become manifest in popular memory. From Chamberlain's 'pawn ticket saved / from the antepenultimate ultimatum' and 'Britannia's own narrow / miracle of survival' 'grudgingly' owned as the work of prewar Polish cryptanalysts, to the shame of the firestorms with their 'well-timed, / intermitted terror' (X, XV and XI), Britain's wartime legend is seen as 'our own tragic satire'.

But what most personally engages the poet is that the enormity of loss and sacrifice has not been honoured and has not been instructive for postwar England:

> By what right did Keyes, or my cousin's
> Lancaster, or the trapped below-decks watch
> of Peter's clangorous old destroyer-escort,
> serve to enfranchise these strange children
> pitiless in their ignorance and contempt?
>
> (LXXVII)

One of the main components of the betrayal of the fallen is again the wholesale conversion of everything into a species of entertainment or spectacle. Hill satirises this at a trivial level in the section that follows an affectionate recollection of Gracie Fields ('her patter still / bright as the basement gents' brass taps at the Town Hall'):

> Sir, your 'Arts/Life' column claims that Gracie
> Fields sang at Dunkirk. Is this
> a misprint? For sang read sank? [Phew,
> what a 'prang'! – ED]
>
> (XLVIII)

The slash conflation of Arts and Life is a sideswipe at the tone of con-
temporary 'serious' arts journalism and its cheap, confusion of the two
based on an avidity for confession. The 'Arts/Life' voice will appear
again in CXXIX:

> One or two illustrations might help us –
> *Geffe* – to take a fix on your position,
> anomalous as it is.

The jokes in these several passages are acute and funny but also savagely
indignant as he goes beyond the quips – 'Incantation or incontinence –
the lyric cry? / Believe me, he's not / told you the half of it. (*All who are
able may stand*.)' (CXLV) – to a vision which sees such obsession as car-
rion feeding:

> *A se stesso*: of Self, the lost cause to end all
> lost causes;
> …
> *Fama/Fame* [It. – ED]: celebrity and hunger
> gorging on road kill. *A se stesso*.
>
> (CXL)

The indignation comes from the obscene disparity between this obses-
sion with the celebrated, inquired after, exposing and self-exposing Self
of contemporary culture and the 'mass-solitariness' of the century's vic-
tims. That breathtaking oxymoron stands at the centre of this short,
quiet section:

> Devouring our names they possess and destroy
> by numbers: the numbered, the numberless
> as graphs of totality pose annihilation.
> Each sensate corpse, in its fatal
> mass-solitariness, excites
> multiples of infliction. A particular
> dull yard on a dull, smoky day. This, and this,
> the unique face, indistinguishable, this, these,
> choked in a cess-pit of leaking Sheol.
>
> (XCVII)

In the numbed, stumbling reiteration of the immensity, here, as in XIII, Hill echoes Whitman's horrified realisation of 'The Million Dead, Too, Summ'd Up' from the prose collection *Specimen Days*: 'the varieties of the *strayed* dead'; and from Pound's terse summations in 'Hugh Selwyn Mauberley (Life and Contacts)': 'There died a myriad'. In surprising contrast to this stark enumeration is another paradox in 'Each sensate corpse'. 'Sensate' can mean 'gifted by sense', 'endowed with sense' and 'perceived by the senses' (*OED*). The expected word is of course its antithesis, 'insensate', but the first layer of meaning achingly underlines the corpses' closeness to sense both of life ('gifted … endowed') and pain, and the second layer the feeling brought by the compelled gaze of the onlooker. In the middle too is the terrible verb 'excites', an obscene tremor – like 'desirable' in 'September Song' – which hints at a vile emotiveness amid the language of computation. But vitally important too is the reminder of singularity, the particular, the unique, and thus the horror of 'indistinguishable' extinction. This is the weight and true significance of individuality – *a se stesso* – to himself.

It might then not seem surprising that *The Triumph of Love* includes a more evidently autobiographical mode than any of his previous work, save perhaps for *Mercian Hymns*. This appears primarily in childhood recollection, coinciding with the war and immediately postwar years. What distinguishes Hill's autobiographical essay however is the complex relation between *memory*, understood as the particular, the unique, which is something essentially inward and part of that selfhood denied his murdered contemporaries, and *Memoria*, as classically understood, the store of inherited knowledge and wisdom, what Brian Vickers calls in his *In Defence of Rhetoric* 'the treasure house of the ideas supplied by Invention'.[4] The voice of memory might be represented by the single line of the poem's opening section: 'Sun-blazed, over Romsley, a livid rain-scarp.' This announces a poem that is 'something other than a conventionally communicative act' (*The New Princeton Encyclopedia of Poetry and Poetics*).[5] By contrast, the section beginning 'Whose lives are hidden in God?' (XIII, see above), is vocative, 'persuasively audience-directed' (*Princeton*). But also, from early in the poem in the section on the bombing of Coventry (VII), the two characters of memory and address are intertwined. Ostensible public memory, that which might and should be *Memoria*, is however seen as ignored or compromised by a selectively amnesiac governance:

> Memory
> and attention died, *comme ça*,
> which is not reasonable. Polity regroups
> and is guarded, where on D-Day men

> drowned by the gross, in surf-dreck, still harnessed
> to their lethal impedimenta.
>
> (CXVI)

Immediately prior to LXXVII, in which the poet rages at the waste of the poet Sidney Keyes and 'my cousin's Lancaster', England is characterised as 'a nation / with so many memorials but no memory' (LXXVI). 'What is to become of memory?' he asks (CXXXVIII). Reluctantly, this dimension of memory is driven back into the personal. Sometimes it is rhetorical in the sense that it is couched in a mode of public address as across CXXXVI–VII,

> We are children
> of the Thirties, the sour dissipation;
> England at once too weepy and too cold.
>
> The glowering carnival: nightly solar-flare
> from the Black Country; minatory beacons
> of ironstone, sulphur. Then, greying, east-northeast,
> Lawrence's wasted pit-villages rising early,
> spinning-wheel gear-iron girding above each
> iron garth; old stanchions wet with field-dew.

Here the images, partly drawing on literary reference, act as synecdoche for industrial England but they are stamped, dependent even, upon the closely observed detail which closes the section, the 'stanchions wet with field-dew'. That unbearable juxtaposition of 'the brute mass and detail of the world' can be pondered because of the acute sense and expression of *detail* that the poem gives us of individual people and of natural and made objects. Such images recur again and again, vivifying the poem, drawing us to recognise such things as 'the barely recognized / beauty of the potato vine in its places / of lowly flowering' (LVIII).

This power is part of the neat, satiric literalising of the cliché 'moral landscape' that goes across LI–LIII. The 'landscape' is first envisaged in geological strata 'in which particular grace, / individual love, decency, endurance, / are traceable across the faults'. Then, in LII, with a touch of self-mockery, Hill characterises his persistent preoccupation as a kind of peculiar tinnitus:

> archaic burrings like a small, high-fenced
> electricity sub-station of uncertain age
> in a field corner where the flies
> gather and old horses shake their sides.

Thus is memory seen and represented as exactly the kind of odd associations and recollections we recognise. But there is an acknowledged pathos here too, for in the succeeding section the poet tugs himself away from this brooding – 'leave it now, leave it' – though that only produces another brilliantly realised recollection, which not only the writer but the reader can enter into, and then concludes with an evocation of

> that all-gathering general English light,
> in which each separate bead
> of drizzle at its own thorn-tip stands
> as revelation.
>
>   (LIII)

This last, phenomenally concentrated image, takes us into another, noumenal realm of thought which contributes to quite different triumphs of realisation, although in one sense it marks a recognition of retreat from a shared currency of memory and recognition.

   Here we have a key issue in the poem's argument, or rather, process, and one that bears not only upon this work but on poetry in this era. Hill announces the poem's participation in public discourse, specifically through '*Laus / et vituperatio*, the worst / remembered, least understood, of the modes' (XXIII). In his *In Defence of Rhetoric*, Brian Vickers writes:

> the Latin translation of Averroës' paraphrase of Aristotle's *Poetics*, which begins 'Every poem and all poetic discourse is blame or praise ... [of] the honourable or the base'; and the techniques of debate in schools and universities, where opposed arguments fell naturally into the moulds of *laus* and *vituperatio*. As a result of these and other influences epideictic [i.e. panegyric] was indissolubly linked with ethical themes, and deeply affected all literary genres. Epic was the form most obviously influenced, with its tendency to divide characters into the polar extremes of virtuous and vicious, but the injunction to make moral discriminations by praise and blame was applied even to lyric. As Ben Jonson said of the poet, 'We do not require in him mere elocution; or an excellent faculty in verse; but the exact knowledge of all virtues, and their contraries; with ability to render the one loved, the other hated, by his proper embattling them.'[6]

A number of important matters relevant to *The Triumph of Love* might be drawn from Vickers's exposition. In espousing rhetoric, specifically *laus et vituperatio*, praise and blame, Hill is pursuing a tradition which places poetry as a part of public discourse, an address to an audience which seeks to make use of its eloquence to persuade. (Vickers quotes Cicero's *De Oratore*: 'the poet is very near kinsman of the orator'.) It aims to be 'public, forensic, / yet with a vehement / private ambition for the people's / greater good' (XXVI). 'Forensic' is a term taken from Aristotle's conception of speaking before judge or jury which 'either attacks or defends somebody'.[7] (Given the prominence in the poem's image-world of burials, 'the false equities of common ash' (XXVI) – one is tempted to call them its exhibits – the more familiar, present-day sense of the term seems also to be in play.) Now this is a high and dangerous ambition, for 'the injunction to make moral discriminations', Jonson's expectation of 'exact knowledge of all virtues, and their contraries' is massively daunting. Moreover it is especially so at this point in history where the task of writing an epic, or finding any story which will demonstrate 'the polar extremes of virtuous and vicious' is all but impossible. The Second World War, the West's central narrative of the twentieth century – especially as mediated to the young, most particularly Hill's generation – is the one that has been granted, and is most likely to justify, such an antithesis. But for Hill it is too compromised, too terrible to serve as an exemplum, its triumph and sacrifice too little understood or followed, our whole 'Progress' indeed too pathetically halting:

> The secular masque, advanced
> by computation, has not otherwise
> progressed. Millennial authority
> makes necromantic the fire-targeted
> century. African new-old
> holocaust suffers up against
> the all-time Hebrew *shoah*.
>
> (CXXIII)

The failures are dyed into our language with its 'technical advance', 'Millennium-overviews' and treatment of such events as Rwanda as a chopping preoccupation with better/worse, same/different from the 'existing record' or 'standard'.

It is in language, specifically the currency of public discourse, that Hill has the greatest task in his 'embattling' of virtue and vice. But to use poetry as rhetoric in the classical sense depends upon the existence of a forum in which to be heard, and upon a mode of discourse sharing common ground. This is precisely what the poem cannot lay claim to, and this in turn becomes one of its major subjects:

> Even now, I tell myself, there is a language
> to which I might speak and which
> would rightly hear me;
> responding with eloquence; in its turn,
> negotiating sense without insult
> given or injury taken.
> Familiar to those who already know it
> elsewhere as justice,
> it is met also in the form of silence.
>
> (XXXV)

There is a temptation to see a conservative nostalgia in this, a notion that there was a time when such writers 'with a vehement / private ambition for the people's / greater good' such as Milton and Wordsworth negotiated as part of an eloquent, rightful public discourse. These would be deserving of praise alongside the stoical victims in the landing-craft and Lancaster and the 'widowed generations' and all bound up with the poet's version of a boyhood idyll to comprise 'a land called Lost / at peace inside our heads' ('Two Chorale-Preludes on Melodies by Paul Celan', *CP* p. 165). But, as he has demonstrated before, in 'An Apology for the Revival of Christian Architecture in England' (*CP* pp. 152-64) and elsewhere, Hill can recognise and realise nostalgia from within its gravitational field without being dragged down by it. Systematically he makes no claim for a golden age or the superiority of any past age: 'England crouched beast-wise' beneath Towton in 1461 ('Funeral Music', *CP* p. 72).

This is not to say that there may not be vision – 'beneath, / Like a revealed mineral, a new earth' ('In Piam Memoriam', *CP* p. 56) – still less that human thought and imagination in religion, art and philosophy have not proffered the ethics and the beauty that might be the means to that vision. One prominent feature of *The Triumph of Love* is the *laus* offered through a large scattering to such figures as Rouault, Aleksander Wat, 'the solitary great ones – Isaiah, Amos / Ezekiel', Rembrandt and Montale. But they come as a scattering, each seized upon as defiance and consolation, and, like previous 'difficult friends' such as Mandelstam and Péguy, they tend to share an embattled position, and achievements that are won by the engraving of effort against the odds. Even his brilliant vignette in tribute to Laurel and Hardy chooses to pick them out 'cutting, pacing, repacing, their / flawless shambles' (CX).

> What remains? You may well ask. Construction
> or deconstruction? There is some poor
> mimicry of choice, whether you build or destroy.
>
> (XXIII)

These figures cannot be gathered into any central, coherent body of reference as might be called, for instance, a 'tradition'. Their triumphs are significant, exemplary and luminous, but they are won and found here and there. To refer back to the epideictic character of *laus et vituperatio*, the clear model of epic with its single virtuous hero and single narrative triumph is not available to the poet of this age.

In this connection it is perhaps significant which literary figures are among Hill's main guides in the poem and which are not: Petronius rather than Virgil, Petrarch rather than Dante. Instead of the secure narrative arch of *The Divine Comedy* with its massive sense of destination, Hill looks to the *rime sparse* – 'scattered verses' – of the Petrarchan sequence. The sections that work most directly from Petrarch and his invocation '*Vergine bella*' move from this highly traditional, even arcane, beginning through a free-form *canzone* of astounding eclecticism and subtlety – see LV, CIX, CXXV, and the mid-point:

> *Vergine bella*, now I am half-way
> and lost – need I say – in this maze of my own
> devising. I would go back and start
> again; or not start at all, which might
> be wiser. No. Delete the last four words.
> Talking to oneself is in fact
> a colloquy with occasion – *eppur*
> *si muove* – or so I tell myself.
>
> (LXXV)

In choosing 'Petronius Arbiter' to 'take us in charge' (III), the disruptive, iconoclastic voice of the satirist is preferred to the even confidence and single voice of the *Aeneid*. Petronius's provocatively outrageous millionaire Trimalchio, Cupidity personified, can plausibly be placed 'among the legends that now circulate / about Canary Wharf, the Isle of Dogs' (L), but it is the roughing-up of the tone, the puncturing and self-puncturing, especially of rhetoric – Petronius's opening target in *The Satyricon* – that Hill can draw upon here: 'Obnoxious chthonic old fart' … 'Shameless old man' … 'Rancorous narcissistic old sod' … 'I may be gone sometime. *Hallelujah!* / Confession and recantation in fridge.'

The satirist's voice in the poem is adjacent to that of *vituperatio*, and indeed the 'splenetics' to which it returns. This is a mode that has engaged Hill before, notably in his essay on Swift, ('Jonathan Swift: the Poetry of "Reaction"', *LL*, 1984, pp. 67-83). As he wryly notes there, 'invective is a touchy subject' (p. 76), and so it has proved in early reactions to *The Triumph of Love*. The celebrated '*N*. and *N*.', the critics

'McSikker', 'O'Shem' and 'Croker' (the last sobriquet comes from one of Keats's assailants whom Hazlitt called 'the talking potato' – the mode is obviously nothing new) are all presumably recognisable although in time their identity will become a parochial matter. At first the *ad hominem*, peevish preoccupation with rivals and reviewers appears unnecessary and demeaning. Why should a poet of Hill's standing care about Grub Street politics, and what place does the argument have in the context of the major events and concerns of the poem? If *The Triumph of Love* is not actually rendering itself unlovely it is certainly taking the risk of being unlovable. But to aim to be accessible, accommodating, ingratiating is, for Hill, to be 'openly servile'. Aside from invoking the long tradition of raillery and invective which includes the vituperative character of Milton's tracts, Dryden, Pope and Swift, the issue is the one Hill poses with regard to Swift: is the invective 'poetically convincing' (*LL* p. 77)? The departure from moderation usually – as in the case of Swift – brings charges of being out of control, though as Hill suggests, the art of invective might include 'deft simulation' of such a condition. The series of parentheses in CXXXIX is a case in point. This section is a strenuous religious meditation 'Concerning wilfulness and determination', occasionally interrupted with '(*eat / shit, MacSikker*) … (*up / yours, O'Shem*)'. The extreme incongruity with the technical seriousness of parts of the meditation, with occasional insouciance – 'It's a Plutarchan twist: even our foes / further us' – and the wrought tributes to Hopkins and Herbert produce a comic effect further underlined by the staginess of the enjambments. But it is also part of a sequence of passages explicitly concerned with the self, 'the lost cause to end all / lost causes' (CXL), including the lines about the 'lyric cry' and confessionalism referred to earlier.

When it is at its most self-revealing poetry always aims to be most appealing, and this is the 'authenticity' that journalism and many readers seek. The voice should therefore be pained and suffering, bleeding upon the thorns of life, but its revelations should still not be unlovely. It should not include any of the spite, jealousy or indignation that can seethe in all but the most nicely governed breast. Hill's riposte to the conventional expectations of the mode is to include and deploy just such emotions, using his mixture of the tradition of savage indignation and contemporary demotic to outbid cosmeticised anguish. In the same way that Petrarch passes from being a morally superior bystander of the Triumph of Love to becoming one of its captives, so Hill's spleen draws him into the middle of the kermesse of literary pride and status. This mood of the poem is meant to discomfit the reader and it does. It is a

dangerous game, reckless with the reader's sympathy, and moreover he
cannot rely on being proved right: '"*Saeva indignatio*" is no guarantee
of verdictive accuracy, or even of perception' ('Our Word Is Our Bond',
LL p. 155). Here Hill is discussing Pound, whose stickling defiance and
savage indignation in such work as Cantos XIV–XVI – 'And the betray-
ers of language / ... ... n and the press gang / And those who had
lied for hire' – is, as in other aspects of the poem, one of his models. But,
as essay and poem make clear, nothing in the power of Pound's rhetoric
exonerates his 'moral offence' (*LL* p. 154). However fierce the vituper-
ation might be it cannot claim any 'vatic privilege' (*LL* p. 155).

> And yes – bugger you, MacSikker et al., – I do
> mourn and resent your desolation of learning:
> *Scientia* that enabled, if it did not secure,
> forms of understanding, far from despicable,
> and furthest now, as they are most despised.
> By understanding I understand diligence
> and attention, appropriately understood
> as actuated self-knowledge, a daily acknowledgement
> of what is owed the dead.
>
> (CXIX)

The propensity for rage – for being 'too much moved by hate ... Oh yes
– much / better out than in' (LXXV) – needs to be understood as 'actu-
ated self-knowledge' and is indeed itself actuated in the process of the
poem. In this passage Hill risks the charge that the blunt dismissal proves
mere animus in order to recuperate, through further risk-taking in the
serious wordplay of 'understanding' 'understand' 'understood' and 'far'
'furthest', a seemingly simple statement which is yet a defiant, even pre-
posterous oxymoron: 'a daily acknowledgement / of what is owed the
dead'. In the previous section he has referred to 'voices pitched exactly',
and the notion of *pitch*, a combination of lexical choice, syntactic
arrangement and rhythmical movement that is exactly commensurate to
the idea and emotion that is being struggled for, is central to Hill's poet-
ics and practice. In CXIX the complex lexical, syntactic and rhythmic
movements of the section take it through different tones up to the insis-
tent, even iambic stresses of the monosyllabic last line. The exact pitch
of this is achieved not only by its own qualities but by the context begun
so tonally differently with 'bugger you, MacSikker et al.'. The *process* of
these lines, which includes the poet's exposure as grumpily pugnacious
and part-poseur, might well be seen as the 'proper embattling' of 'virtues
and their contraries' that Jonson writes of.

> I know places where grief has stood mute-
> howling for half a century[.]
>
> (LXXVII)

Yet what is the virtue of acknowledging 'what is owed the dead'? Where
is the sense in the paradox? How can a debt be paid to those who cannot
receive it? Would this not be what is known as an empty gesture? How
can the dead hold us to account?

To ponder this let us consider what would be the implications of
saying that we should pay no attention to the dead. This would mean
that at every point we should turn our back upon on who or whatever
ceases to have a charge upon us, or indeed upon all who have no means
to exert that charge, to make it stick. It is a view of human relations
defined by contract in which if someone can no longer enforce their side
of the contract we are released, exonerated, in the clear. The only oblig-
ation we have is one that is chargeable, for which we can be arraigned.
This is the pragmatism Hill puts before us in his epigraph from the
Amores to 'Ovid in the Third Reich': '*non peccat, quaecumquae potest
pecasse negare, / solaque famosam culpa professa facit*' ('whoever can deny
wrongdoing is innocent; only those who own up are guilty'). The abjec-
tion of guilt known only to the perpetrator does not exist. He who can
keep himself so intact, without memory or guilt, bears a striking resem-
blance to Nietzsche's 'last man' in *Thus Spoke Zarathrustra*: 'Alas! The
time of the most contemptible man is coming, the man that can no
longer despise himself.'[8]

Memory, attention and guilt are bound closely together in *The
Triumph of Love*. After the single-line evocation of Romsley in the open-
ing section we have:

> Guilts were incurred in that place, now I am convinced:
> self-molestation of the child-soul, would that be it?
>
> (II)

This is the realm of *Mercian Hymns*, the obnoxious schoolboy flaying the
hapless 'Ceolred' (*MH* VII) and doing harm to himself by being a soli-
tary and inward boy.

> Go back to Romsley, pick up the pieces, becomes
> a somewhat unhappy figure. I speak
> deliberately like an old man who last saw it –
> Romsley – through a spinning bike-wheel, as indeed
> Kenelm may have done.
>
> ...

> High swine-pasture it was,
> long before Domesday; and will be again,
> albeit briefly, at the flash of Judgement.
> Let it now take for good a bad part of my
> childself. I gather I was a real swine.
>
> (LXXXII)

Here again the passage touches upon a remarkable range of registers. 'Go back to' comes after a splenetic outburst at N. and N. in the previous section and might be peaceable retrenchment, or might – 'pick up the pieces' – be a board-game instruction. 'Becomes / a somewhat unhappy figure' then mimics the style of biographical summary and the deliberation of the old man is underlined by the pedantic superfluous reiteration of Romsley. The 'spinning bike-wheel' flashes the quiddity of particular memory momentarily before us. The section concludes with a colloquial sense of Domesday, and, given the reference to place, its Book, and the revelation of the Last Judgement. The pun on 'for good' signals the speaker's resignation, then slyly winked at by the use of 'I gather', the familiar phrase of recovered memory. But while 'obnoxious' is routinely attached to small boys, it has older meanings: 'exposed to harm … liable to punishment … reprehensible … answerable, amenable (*to* some authority) … submissive … obsequious' (*OED*).

> Obnoxious means, far back within itself,
> easily wounded. But vulnerable, proud
> anger is, I find, a related self
> of covetousness. I came late
> to seeing that. Actually, I had to be
> shown it. What I saw was rough, and still
> pains me. Perhaps it should pain me more.
> Pride is our crux: be angry, but not proud
> where that means vainglorious.
>
> (CXLVIII)

The poet, from the 'childsoul' to 'the real swine' to the vituperator to the proud self-flagellator – 'Why do I / take as my gift a wounded and wounding / introspection' (LXVII) – and on to this humbled voice pegged on the crux of pride is 'obnoxious' in both senses, and frequently 'obstinate': 'Obstinate old man – *senex / sapiens*, it is not' (V). The lumpish morpheme '*ob-*' – obnoxious, obstinate, oblation, oblivion – with its veins of gaucherie and mulishness seems to recur: a glob signalling the poem's contention with obstruction and its obduracy. Beneath it all is the awareness of the life-span, 'foreplay' in the context of eternity:

> Ever more protracted foreplay,
> never ending – *o ewigkeit* – no act
> the act of oblivion, the blown
> aorta pelting out blood.
>
> (IV)

The whole poem is an act of oblation offered for guilts incurred, and these include the private, the open excesses of vainglory and the guilt of the bystander of the wars, the camps and industrial attrition.

Hard by guilt and responsibility comes the matter of choice and determination: 'What choice do you have? These are false questions. / Fear is your absolute' (LXIX). Fear, as of history's many bloody questions which gentlemen and women of England of the last two generations have largely been fortunate enough to escape – we have missed a throe (XC) – should be confessed to as an absolute. Thus part of what Hill sees to be owed to the dead is the ethical responsibility to confront the question in imagination, and this has been a recurrent theme in his work. The falsity or otherwise of the question depends upon determination. The half-way point in *The Triumph of Love* – 'half-way / and lost' – is reached with these stunning lines in which the tactile ordinariness of the opening image gives the philosophical concept a virtually physical force:

> Corner to corner, the careful
> fabric of our lives ripped through
> by the steel claws of contingency. We are made
> to make ourselves instruments
> of violence and cunning. There seems no
> hook on which we are not caught
> except, by lot, those of the thorns and nails.
>
> (LXXV)

The issue of contingency and free will are considered in theological terms. One point of reference is the obscure Thomas Bradwardine, Archbishop of Canterbury, *ob.* 1349: 'I should hold for my own ... the *De Causa Dei* of Thomas Bradwardine' (VIII). Bradwardine's work was a confutation of the often-named 'English heresy' of Pelagianism. Followers of Pelagius denied the transmission of original sin, claiming that, unaffected by the Fall, man can do all that God commands and take the road to salvation of his own volition: 'if I ought I can'. The consequent denial of the need for baptism and divine grace led Augustine to have the doctrine first declared heretical in 416 AD. However, the rejection of original sin and the opportunity for

self-making made some versions of Pelagian doctrines recurrently pop-
ular and its tenets have contributed to rationalist-humanist critiques of
traditional Christianity.[9]

Apparently liberating at first, it is however easy to see how forbid-
ding a challenge it presents. If strong versions of Calvinism could terrify
adherents by insistence upon the inescapability of original sin and the
scarcity of election and grace, then, conversley, the Pelagian view could
overwhelm by the freedom it offers to escape 'the steel claws of contin-
gency' and live virtuously. Whilst to contemporary readers such disputa-
tion might appear obfuscatory, obnoxious even, it is not difficult to see
how its lineaments are translated into secular terms. Contingency and
choice, 'wilfulness and determination' (CXXXIX), are the crux of all eth-
ical, and thus political questions. Confronting bloody questions we stand
before judgement and are in need of mercy.

Judgement implies truth – 'verdictive accuracy'. Verdicts can be
delivered only in language. In his discussion of J. L. Austin in 'Our Word
Is Our Bond' (*LL* pp. 138-59), Hill tested the philosopher's rigorous
quest to purge language of opacities and achieve a transparent identity
of word and deed. Whilst arguing that the 'play' in language is ineradi-
cable and a condition with which we must deal, he does still honour
Austin's attachment of responsibility to speech, not least for the poet. In
CXXV of *The Triumph of Love* Hill adduces Wittgenstein, who early in
the *Tractatus Logico-Philosophicus* (1922)[10] asserts that

> Most of the propositions and questions of philosophers arise from
> our failure to understand the logic of our language … And it is not
> surprising that the deepest problems are in fact *not* problems at all.
> (4.003)

'All philosophy', he continues, 'is a "critique of language"' (4.0031).
Later, Wittgenstein describes the aim of logical proof: 'Proof in logic is
merely a mechanical expedient to facilitate the recognition of tautologies
in complicated cases' (6.1262). A tautology is an equation in which both
sides are identified, a proposition that is 'true for all the truth-possibilities
of the elementary propositions' (4.46). Thus logic is the procedure which,
lacking all content or sense itself, can bring us to recognise truth, even in
'complicated cases'. 'Logic', Wittgenstein continues in 6.13, 'is transcen-
dental.' 'The logic of the world, which is shown in tautologies by the
propositions of logic, is shown in equations by mathematics' (6.22).

The attraction of Wittgenstein's thesis must be that the welter of
'complicated cases' that comprise the world we know is subject to a tran-
scendent that we can conceive and apply, that 'mathematics is a logical

method' (6.2), and as that logical method is applied to the underlying structures of language so we shall be able to see what is true. (There is perhaps an interesting and cognate linguistic issue concerning the word '*case*' and its etymology in the Latin '*casus*' which includes the meaning '*fall*'. The famous opening sentence of the *Tractatus* is '*Die Welt ist alles, was der Fall ist*', usually translated as 'The world is all that is the case'. The deliberately neutral tenor of '*case*' in English tends to disguise what must be covered by a phrase like 'complicated cases'. In the present context, the connotations coming from the German '*Fall*' might extend beyond such an alternative translation as 'The world is all that befalls'.)

There may too be an exciting strangeness in that a tautology can also be said to say nothing. In CXXV Hill finds this strange:

> Estrangement itself
> is strange, though less so than the metaphysics
> of tautology, which is at once *vain*
> *repetition* and *the logic of the world*
> [Wittgenstein] ...
> Then there is this
> Augustinian-Pascalian thing about seeking
> that which is already found. Tautology
> for Wittgenstein, manifests the condition
> of unconditional truth. Mysticism is not
> affects but grammar. There is nothing
> mysterious in grammar; it constitutes
> its own mystery, its *practicum*.

Against Wittgenstein's transcendent Hill poses Bradwardine:

> The intellectual
> beauty of Bradwardine's thesis rests
> in what it springs from: the Creator's grace
> *praecedentem tempore et natura* ['Strewth!!!
> 'already present in time as in nature'? – ED]
> and in what it returns to – our arrival
> at a necessary salvation. So much
> for the good news.

Both thinkers seek a ground, truth, and for both it is 'already present'. Bradwardine's assertion of 'the Creator's grace' is relief in the face of the Pelagian field of free will and responsibility – 'the good news'. The section then continues with the case against Christianity and the Church: 'guaranteed / damnation for dead children unbaptized ... the unending

negotium, / the expediencies, enforcements, and rigged evidence' but
concluding with a hard-won, stubborn reiteration of Bradwardine:

> I have been working up to this. The Scholastics
> mean more to me than the New Science. All
> things are eternally present in time and nature.

This, despite admitting previously, in CIX, that 'many, perhaps most, /
would argue against the relevance / of the Scholastics', and acknowl-
edging 'the New Science' in the 'signal / mystery, mercy' of serotonin.
No matter what grace 'the conversion or / reconversion of brain chem-
icals' provides, it is, this section argues, no exoneration from 'our ulti-
mate reprobation', nor from our commitment 'to loving / desperately,
yet not with despair, not / even in desperation'.

Thus Wittgenstein's mysticism is not seen as transcendent but, as
grammar, language, a science that is part of the earthly *practicum* and
negotium. Nevertheless, as we shall see, there are succeeding parts of the
Tractatus that may be more sympathetic to Hill's vision.

But how might Bradwardine's version of presence be apprehended?
Might it be dismissed as 'affects', indeed an affect of language? Section
XXXVIII is a place to consider this:

> Widely established yet with particular
> local intensities, the snow
> half-thawed now hardens over again,
> glassen-ridged, or pashed
> like fish-ice: refracted light
> red against copper. The hedged sun
> draws into itself for its self-quenching.
> If one is so minded, these modalities
> stoop to re-enter the subterrane of faith –
> faith, that is, in real Being;
> the real being God or, more comprehensively, Christ – [.]

The section begins with the diurnal, generalising phraseology of weather
forecasts – 'widely-established ... local intensities' – and then produces
this vividly specific detailed image of the snow moving between thaw and
frozen, 'glassen' and 'pashed' both impressing by their onomatopoeic
effect and by the sense of close locality – a real local intensity – that comes
from the use of dialect words. It is a minute, fleeting but utterly realised
epiphany. These changes of snow and light are then abstractly named as
'modalities'. This is because we see their different modes, but also to con-
note 'modality', a term used, the philosopher tells us, to describe the way
in which a proposition is true or false drawn from scholastic logic in

which a 'mode' is 'a determination, a focusing of being in the abstract into some specific form'.[11] In the snow-ice and sunlight the poet apprehends 'real Being'. Moments of exact natural description elsewhere describe the same experience, for instance in IX: 'On chance occasions – / ... you can see the wind ... It is how / the purest apprehension might appear / to take corporeal shape'. This, for Hill, is the kind of 'modality' which shows him 'the Creator's grace ... "already present in time as in nature"'.

The colloquy with Wittgenstein might however be seen to go further. In the closing pages of the *Tractatus*, from proposition 6.4 onwards, the philosopher is addressing the limits of apprehension and how far our words can reach. What might be called mystical in this phase of his thought is that while he circumscribes the limits of any proposition we can make –

> 6.41 The sense of the world must lie outside the world ...

> 6.42 And so it is impossible for there to be propositions of ethics. / / Propositions can express nothing of what is higher.

> 6.421 It is clear that ethics cannot be put into words. / / Ethics is transcendental. / / (Ethics and aesthetics are one and the same.)

– he does insist upon something that lies outside the world, 'of what is higher'. In the succeeding sequence, which begins with a commentary on death, Wittgenstein writes:

> 6.432 *How* things are in the world is a matter of complete indifference for what is higher. God does not reveal himself *in* the world.

> 6.4321 The facts all contribute only to setting the problem, not to its solution.

> 6.44 It is not *how* things are in the world that is mystical, but *that* it exists.

In the 'glassen-ridged' ice, the 'roiling plug of sand', in the poem's opening image, 'Sun-blazed, over Romsley, a livid rain-scarp', is Hill's realised sense of marvel *that* the world exists.

But although the poem begins and ends 'over Romsley' it has not remained in that revealed moment. If this is such a noumenal vision, a 'mystical' thing such as Wittgenstein says 'cannot be put into words', one such as '*make themselves manifest*' (6.522), Hill does not stop with touching the '*that*'. This sense is important because it is perceived and gathers meaning to itself. It moves from being 'a livid rain-scarp' in the

first poem to '*the* livid rain-scarp' (my emphasis) in the last, that is to
being a constituent of an individual human memory, perhaps too elu-
sively personal for the reader's full grasp, but indicative of just that kind
of intimation. Petrarch's *Trionfo* begins in the glare of Phoebus, and
there is something minatory, even aggressive in the image: 'blazed ...
livid', and following and preceding its two occurrences is the preoccu-
pation with guilt and forgiveness. Ethics for Hill, even if transcendent,
are a part of *how* things are in the world, its *practicum* and *negotium*. The
sense of self is precious – and it is selfhood which is most obscenely
denied in the century's losses – but it is also a burden of consciousness
and responsibility. The articulation of this is where aesthetics must match
ethics in the quest for perfect pitch. 'We are immortal' in the sense that
there is no escape from this: 'All / things are eternally present in time
and nature': 'Tomorrow he died, became war-dead, picked / off the sky's
face' (LXXVIII). The poem is a great act of oblation in the face of 'the
act of oblivion'. Its triumph is in the strenuous lovingness of the atten-
tion with which this act is conducted.

8 'Beauty is difficult': Speech! Speech! (2000)

In a seminar discussion following a performance of Alban Berg, I recall a member of the Lindsay String Quartet saying that, unlike all that had gone before, modern music 'is allowed to be ugly'.

'Beauty' might indeed be said to be a problem for many twentieth-century artists. In his essay on Ezra Pound's 'Envoi (1919)' in *The Enemy's Country* Geoffrey Hill quotes Pound's assertion 'Beauty is difficult' (*EC* p. 96), a quotation from the first of the 'Pisan Cantos', LXXIV:

> Beloved the hours βροδοδάκτυλος
>   as against the half-light of the window
>   with the sea beyond making horizon
> le contre-jour the line of the cameo
> profile 'to carve Achaia'
>   a dream passing over the face in the half-light
>   Venere, Cytherea 'aut Rhodon'
>   vento ligure, veni
> 'beauty is difficult' sd / Mr Beardsley
> beauty is difficult
> in the days of the Berlin to Bagdad [*sic*] project[1]

and the phrase is reiterated as the passage proceeds. The image of the dawn, its half-light, 'le contre-jour', is an evocation of the beauty of the natural world and includes the slow drowsiness of the long cadence, 'a dream passing over the face in the half-light'. But the ease of this sensuous pleasure is intermitted by stoppages in the rhythm and diction, and the reflexiveness that comes with, in the first instance, attributing the key phrase: '"beauty is difficult" sd / Mr Beardsley'. It is difficult moreover 'in the days of the Berlin to Bagdad project', that is under the pressure of political and economic events.

With these lines in mind I go to the bridge between two sections in Hill's *Speech! Speech!* , sections 80 and 81:

> Even today the light
> is beautiful – you can hardly avoid
> seeing thát: shadows – reflections – on reeds
> and grasses | deepening visibility:
> the mind's invisible cold conflagration.
>
> 81
> Again: the saltmarsh in winter. By dawn
> drain-mouths grow yellow beards. Old man's duty,
> vigilance so engrained, shabby observance,
> dirty habit, wavelets chinning the shore-line.
> Rich in decrepit analogues | he sees:
> archipelagos, collops of sewage,
> wormed ribs jutting through rime.

This passage begins with one of those moments when Hill responds to our desire for naturalisation, and for 'the poetic': a clear, lyrical evocation of natural beauty. But then he moves into an equally perfectly observed ugliness as the waterscape resolves into the stains of pollution. The 'collops of sewage' are particularly repulsive. A 'collop' from its sound has the connotation of 'dollop', a 'clumsy shapeless lump' (*OED*), and the specific reference to a dish of fried egg on bacon.

Literary modernism had eschewed what Pound called 'mellifluous archaism',[2] and Charles Olson dismissed as 'the sweetness of meter and rime in a honey-head' [3] of traditional cadences. At this point it is as well to recap the now familiar set of characteristics of modernism with regard to poetic style. First is the determination to disrupt the predominantly iambic traditional verse-line, 'to break the pentameter, that was the first heave' as Pound recalled in Canto LXXXI. Second was the effort to disrupt the lyric 'I' with its presumptions of unified consciousness and a single speaking voice. Hence the conception of impersonality as expounded in Eliot's essay 'Tradition and the Individual Talent', and the development of the *persona*. As Pound puts it: 'In "the search for one-self", in the search for "sincere self-expression", one gropes, one finds, for some seeming verity. One says "I am" this that or the other, and with the words scarcely uttered one ceases to be that thing.'[4] Thirdly there is the replacement of narrative, and indeed consecutive conscious thought, by sequence and juxtaposition, though by a procedure that must, according to Pound, 'juxtapose with science'. At a further extreme of this challenge to conventional discursiveness is the anti-rationalism of manifesto Surrealism. In general all these contribute to what Alan Wall has described as:

literally breaking the surface of the poem, by fissuring narrative, authorial focus, temporal coherence, unity of voice, or the parameters of one dictionary. History intruded with its cinematic cuts, jabbering away in languages living and dead, constantly interrupting itself in different voices.[5]

This roughing-up element of modernism has become more and more evident in Hill's later work – especially in *Speech! Speech!* – and it is on this quality that I want to concentrate here.

These features of modernism have resulted in a different kind of reading and criticism in the twentieth century which has been applied to a great variety of texts. Procedures are no longer narrative but pattern-seeking, exploring for instance the coincidence of imagery, and so establishing a different kind of thread to replace narrative. The philosopher Charles Taylor writes 'We triangulate to the meaning [of e.g. Eliot's 'Prufrock'] through the images', and quotes Roger Shattuck on how 'criticism in all the arts has settled on the term "juxtaposition" "to convey the idea of how the parts of a modern work of art are put together"'.[6] The risk of such a proceeding may become idiosyncratic, even casual, but this is the style of reading of *Speech! Speech!* I'm attempting here.

In *Speech! Speech!* Wall's description is seen at an extreme. The sequence is a cacophony of different voices: meditative, speech-making, comic strip, stage-comic, cliché, advertising and other branches of performance and the media. All appear in a cut-and-paste of to-do lists, post-its, diary jottings, imperatives, real and imaginary dialogues, obits, mishearings – often incongruously funny like the mistaking of 'credo' for 'car-radio'. It is, as we say, what is 'in the air', but a performance that can sound like static, or the product of the frantic, irritated twiddling of a radio-tuner. Reference to radio and radio programmes recur, usually in terms of poor reception: 'the sputtering agents of Marconi' (2); 'Strengthen your signal I AM LOSING YOU' (5); 'That's nót WORKERS' PLAYTIME' (17); 'Try Hilversum' (23), 'Daventry and Droitwich / are still transmitting' (105) and many others. This crucial aural dimension is pointed by the dedication to David Wright, poet and friend of Hill's, who was himself deaf. Poem 25 memorialises Wright and evokes the contemporary musician Evelyn Glennie:

> As I believe I heard I the astounding
> percussionist is deaf. David said once
> he could draw music up through heel of hand
> (not Saul's David; David of DEAFNESS, late,
> silenced by throat cancer) though the instrument
> in this connection was indeed a harp.

The other stylistic model is caricature. One of Honoré Daumier's *Croquis pris au théâtre* is Hill's choice for his cover, and Daumier's sketch of a gormlessly applauding audience with its caustically ironic caption, '*On dit que les Parisiens sont difficiles à satisfaire, sur ces quatre banquettes pas un mécontent – il est vrai que tous ces Français sont des Romains*', is the image for Hill's view of the uncritical sycophancy that is part of the soundtrack of contemporary culture.[7] 'Speech! Speech!' they cry. The manner of the *croquis*, a swift, rough sketch, is emulated in the brief, mobile sections of *Speech! Speech!* which Hill has said, in a radio interview, should be read at pace. The visual parallels are dominated by Daumier's method in both his *croquis* and his rough 'sculptures' with their appearance of a child's plasticine modelling, his 'goúged, / wrenched, and sagging clay' (120). Woodcuts and rough work, from the engravings of Jacques Callot to the scrap material and heavy impasto of the canvases of the contemporary painter Anselm Kiefer, are recalled in poems that are themselves a sort of crayoning or 'clown-painting' (11). It is a style of gargoyle caricature that fits Hill's satiric purpose.

Taken together, the polyphonic 'static' of surrounding 'speech' and the *bricolage* of rough imagery comprise an overwhelming collage. What Hill is concerned with is 'discourse' and/or 'the culture', though such conventional summary terms are certainly sucked into this *dictionnaire des idées reçues*. But it is not analytic in the way of a dictionary, but really a satiric, often pantomimic performance of contemporary rhetoric.

These aural and visual stylistic influences of distortion and dissolution are fit for the time and are of the time. Crucially both seem to diminish individual integrity: how can an independently individual voice make itself heard in the din that occupies and drowns it, and how can these cartooned stereotypes correspond to the complexity of real people? To point up its disgust and its fears, satire deals roughly. Its indicted image is the result of the rude stopping of its focal length. The danger of satire is that it might not recover from its own distortions. Satire's perennial complaint is that people are so in thrall to the trivial, the sensual, the spectacular, that they have lost all identity as moral beings. For Dietrich Bonhoeffer – whose temper seems to me not in the least satirical – the defining condition of modernity is that human beings have become 'religionless', by which he means not just that they have ceased to subscribe to religious belief and practice, but that 'the time of inwardness and conscience' is over.[8] Thus, despairing, the contented satirist 'turns away in disgust'. But Hill is not a contented satirist. The task of his poem is to register the force of din and distortion – indeed enact it – but also to articulate and to see the human eye in the poked socket of the clay. Working with some images, I want to continue by following Hill's search for 'inwardness and conscience' in the cacophony and collage of the modern world.

In the first of his Tanner Lectures, on the nature of value,[9] Hill quotes from Sermon VI of the eighteenth-century English divine Joseph Butler:

> *Lastly*, the various miseries of life which lie before us wherever we turn our eyes, the frailty of this mortal state we are passing through, may put us in mind that the present world is not our home; that we are merely strangers in it, as our fathers were.

Hill continues

> And so, for Butler, I would say, 'our ignorance, the imperfection of our nature, our virtue and our condition in this world' are intrinsic to our creatureliness: notice, in the words I have just quoted (from the beginning of Sermon XIV) how 'virtue' is not lacking but is found together *with* 'our ignorance' and 'the imperfection of our nature'.

Reading this at the same time as *Speech! Speech!* my eye was caught by Butler's 'wherever we turn our eyes'. One episode that recurs sporadically in Hill's book is of the civil war in Nigeria in 1966–7.[10] This is section 19:

> For stately archaic detail | tag Dürer's
> LORD MORLEY with POMEGRANATE: self-shielding,
> facet-compacted, its glitter-heart scarce-
> broken | FIDUCIA. Go easy: think GRENADE.
> Faithfulness wrong-footed (this, now, in re
> Colonel F. Fajuyi, late Nigerian Army)
> asks and receives praise-songs in lieu. The sun
> scans Cancer to Capricorn: emergent
> cohorts | mass for mutation. Semiotics
> rule | semiautomatics: is the surreal
> any more our defence? Call the tribunals
> to order | but not right now.

The passage works with an association of ideas and wordplay, especially based on misprision. As the *OED* tells us, the common element of *granate* takes us from pomegranate to grenade, an accident of polysemy where words first seem to relate to words not things. Then too there is the connotation in which 'emergent' calls to mind the familiar locution

of 'emergent nations'. Behind 'mass for mutation' stands the rhetoric of
the era, especially Prime Minister Harold Macmillan's famous speech in
1960 about 'the wind of change' sweeping Africa, but 'mutation' is too
close to 'mutilation', and then to mass graves. This 'play' is then under-
lined with reflexive irony in the sardonic pun: 'semiotics / rule | semiau-
tomatics' in which 'rule' may also hint at linguistic rule. Indeed such rule
does not govern weapons, save in the field where words respond to
words.

This serious setting of the disparities of words and events is a famil-
iar theme in Hill's poetry, one explored critically in his essay 'Our Word
Is Our Bond' (*LL* pp. 138–59). This rueful semiotic play encourages a
vision of the world as a chaos where meanings are so cross-wired as to
carry no import. To invoke another species of distortion, as we com-
monly say: 'it's surreal'.

When we do say this it is one of the ways by which we signal confu-
sion, or a dismissal that might be derisive or resigned. The world does
not seem to us subject to either rationality or ethics. But where does the
defeat of reason and ethical responsibility take us? Like the death camps
of Europe, the cruelties of the Nigerian civil wars were 'surreal'. In sec-
tion 21 Hill looks at this use of the term:

> SURREAL is natural | só you can discount
> ethics and suchlike. Try perpetuity
> *in vitro*, find out how far is HOW FAR.
> I'd call that self | inflicted. Pitch it
> to the CHORUS like admonition. Stoics
> have answers, but nót one I go for.
> Think surreal | the loss of peripheral
> vision vis-à-vis conduct. See if Í care
> any less than did Desnos, but he cannot
> now be recovered | sight unseen. Body
> language my eye. Regarding the shrimp
> as predator: EYE TO EYE IT IS TRUE.

But 'is the surreal / any more our defence?' Does an assertion that the
'surreal' is the natural state of affairs relieve us of bothering with 'ethics
and suchlike'? The fate of the one-time surrealist poet Robert Desnos in
the concentration camp of Terezin in 1944 – as in Hill's earlier poem on
him, 'Domaine Public' (*King Log*; *CP* p. 80) – represents an eruption of
the real into the imaginary, or of the viciousness of the imaginary into
the real – '"Christ what a pantomime!"' The eye, what we see before us,
is prominent in 21: Desnos has gone out of sight,

> cannot
> now be recovered | sight unseen. Body
> language my eye. Regarding the shrimp
> as predator: EYE TO EYE IT IS TRUE.

In this context, the modish concept of 'body language' might have altogether heavier connotations, hence its punning, mocking dismissal. The sense of bodily suffering is intense in 'Domaine Public' where Hill imagines Desnos recommending, bitterly and ironically, the Church Fathers' mortification of 'the corrupting flesh:

> toothsome contemplation: cleanly
>   maggots churning spleen
> to milk.

The corruption works in a double sense: both where its pleasures are held to be corrupt and where it is decaying. The latter sense perhaps can be associated with Desnos's own lines in '10 juin 1936':

> Tous deux pourrissent dans la terre,
> Mordus par les vers sincères.
> La terre emplit leur bouche pour les faire taire.[11]

Like these worms, we must recognise that 'in nature' the toothsome shrimp, with its disproportionate, bulbous eye, takes its part in the disinterested chain of predation.

In section 49 we are taken back to Nigeria:

> Not to forget Colonel Fajuyi, dead
> before I arrived (having lost out to Customs).
> Thát means I was robbed; a sweat-pulped cache
> of small ten-shilling notes (Nigerian). He
> had wórse thíngs to contend with. I don't doubt
> his courage, his slow dying – smell my fear! –
> protracted hide and seek to the bushed kill. Faithful's
> death was as foul but he | went like Elijah.
> Remaindered UN helmets, weapons, fatigues,
> show up here, neo-tribal. Where did you
> ditch the platoon? What have they done with Major
> Nzeogwu's eyes?

Spliced into this is a fragment of autobiography as Hill recalls his own arrival in Nigeria at about this time. The apparently casual remark that Fajuyi had 'wórse thíngs to contend with' in fact takes us towards one of Hill's major themes. From his untested vantage point – 'smell my fear!

– Hill has always been transfixed by comparative comfort, the 'moral luck' of immunity from adjacent suffering. Here he finds himself in the nearly comic, stereotyped role of ripped-off tourist, hot and bothered, realising the gravity of what he is stepping into. The switchback confusion of the Nigerian–Biafran civil war in 1966–67 with its coups, captures and betrayals, its reciprocity of cruelty and occasional honourable stands, are represented in these lurid stories: Fujuyi executed by being forced to crawl through the bush as quarry, and Nzeogwu's body returned without his eyes. 'Surreal or what?' We are defended against these horrors first by the forced jocularity of 'hide and seek', and 'where did you ditch the platoon', where the ditch is all too literal. But then the shock enjambment of the ending tears this away to reveal the raw, hideous physicality that no stance of irony can deal with.

The imagery of sight begins another 'Nigerian' section, 87:

> If I could once focus – Rimbaud's career,
> Nigerian careerists – on a single factor,
> self-centre of anomie, I might present
> to the examiners in whose shadow I am,
> a plainly disordered thesis which they
> must receive to reject: indifferent
> drummers-up for all markets. BIAFRA RULES.
> That long-dead young Igbo master who transferred –
> so abruptly – his panache and command-flag
> from Latin eclogue, from Ovid's *Amores*,
> to POLITICS, ESPIONAGE, AND TRAVEL died
> with or without judgement. Style undisputed.

The whole of *Speech! Speech!* does not 'focus'. In fact it careers about, for example between Rimbaud and the Nigerian civil wars. So many analyses begin 'if there is one single factor that …', but Hill shows the limits of explanatory power, either within the self or in the world beyond. None the less an ordered thesis is expected, not only by the feed examiners of worldly institutions but by a higher standard. What for example were the rights and wrongs of Biafran secession and the Nigerian civil wars? The graffito slogan 'BIAFRA RULES' will not serve as judgement. The tourist can go home, or we can turn the newspaper page. We are not put on the spot, but can remain suspended without pain in our *aporia*. Not so, for instance, the 'long-dead young Igbo master' (Christopher Okigbo, to whom Hill dedicates 'Ezekiel's Wheel' in *Canaan* pp. 56–9) who died in the same battle as Nzeogwu, 'with or without judgement'. In one sense that means without due process, but it also raises other notions of

judgement. Is he to be 'judged' for abandoning poetry for POLITICS, ESPI-
ONAGE, AND TRAVEL, all capitalised as though reified into newspaper sec-
tions. There is such elegiac romance admitted in 'that long-dead young
Igbo master', a phrase redolent of Renaissance aestheticism. But, more
deeply, might judgement also be reached, or at least exercised, regard-
ing what he may or may not have done or achieved politically, or mili-
tarily? For what did he commit himself? Behind this, emerging from
peripheral vision is 'conduct', 'ethics and suchlike', and of course, on
what 'single factor' might the Last Judgement turn. Style may be 'undis-
puted' – though from what we know of Nzeogwu's and Fajuyi's deaths
it seems unlikely that Okigbo could have remained stylish to the end –
but judgement is a different matter, though an unavoidable one.

It is not helped however by continual confusion in language:

> Hów many móre times? Customs not customs!
> Fajuyi was dead by then, though Major Nzeogwu
> still had his eyes. Can't you read English? What
> do I meán by praise-songs? I could weep.
> Thís is a praise-song. These are songs of praise.
> Shall I hyphenate-fór-you? Syntax
> is a dead language, your incoherence
> the volatility of a dead age –
> vintage Brook Farm, adulterate founders' bin;
> and yoú the *faex Rómuli* | the dregs.
> AUTHENTIC SELF a stinker; pass it on,
> *nasum in ano* | the contagious circles.
>
> (99)

His time in Ibadan, Nigeria, 1966–67, was evidently a signal experience
for Hill, but how impure, embattled – jostled – it is in the surrounding
din and uncertainty. If there is a praise-song to be written – and, with
Ezra Pound, Hill sees affirmation, love, praise, veneration as part of
poetry's task – it can fall into routine, saccharine 'songs of praise'. Also,
within the dangerous obscurities of politics and war, where is the knowl-
edge and certainty on which to base praise or judgement? The fragmen-
tary nature of the poet's recollections is a model of this. In his first Tanner
Lecture Hill dwells upon the recurrence of the phrase in both Butler and
Hooker – noted by George Eliot in her reading of Butler – 'for aught we
know'. The extent of our knowledge is not to be taken for granted, even
if one can say 'I was there.'

We might see the Nigerian sections as in part at least authenticated by
the poet's autobiographical involvement. But 'AUTHENTIC SELF a stinker',

says the headline, and the gossip is passed on in the manner of schoolboys' snide whispering. This crude dismissal of the cliché of the 'authentic self' looks sidelong at the historical claims of the lyrical I, and, by implication, at the modernist doctrine of impersonality. But the classroom smuttiness of *nasum in ano*, which is immediately mixed up with the fascinated paranoias of disease, and 'the contagious circles' can be taken as ringworm, a once-feared, highly stigmatic condition in schools, points to how *bodily* the self is. It is a stinker because it is smelly and it lets us down.

The comic confusion of the ending of 99, especially of *nasum in ano*, can be associated with an earlier passage in 51. This, following the worryings of old men in 50, goes from the war recollections and the outrage 'ripped loose / from the vast scope and body of SORROW' to a black comedy of ships sunk by their own torpedoes, of enemas, and rectal examinations:

> Enemas *de rigueur*: no
> mud in the proctologist's third eye; no glycol
> jellying his windshield. Nów he expatiates.
> POSTERITY | how daring! Waste of effort?
> You may conclude so. I do not
> so understand it. Yoú may
> write this off | but it shall not be read so.

In the darkly comic tone and manner of this part of the poem, the phrase 'our/your own worst enema' might be suspected as a submerged pun. His version of the *nasum in ano*, 'the proctologist's third eye', expatiates, that is wanders at will, a word specifically used of eye and hand (*OED*). Then from the posterior we go to POSTERITY – a 'daring' switch we might 'daringly' associate with section 89: 'Don't overstretch it, asshole'. But to bother with the idea of posterity, which must incur judgement, is yet more daring, even though it might be scorned as 'waste of effort'. Other sections (89, 64) recur to the serio-comic experience of rectal examination, 'spitted / up to – and beyond – the caecum', with its 'free ín-house video' (64). The caecum is also known as the blind gut. Insistently, the self, represented above all by the eye, is bodily, especially in its pains and humiliations. In 64, laid out on the proctologist's couch, the poet muses:

> Lift-off but no window. Leibniz's
> monad is one thing. Óne thing or another –
> we are altogether sómething else agaín.

Hill puns upon Leibniz's concept of the monad as a singularity that is self-sufficient, relationless, and therefore 'windowless'. The philosopher

C. S. Pierce, whom Hill draws on in *The Triumph of Love* (XXV), expands
upon the concept of the monad thus:

> Now in order to convert that psychological or logical conception
> into a metaphysical one, we must think of a metaphysical monad as
> a pure nature, or quality, in itself without parts or features, and
> without embodiment. (citation: 'monad', *OED*)

'Spitted up to – and beyond – the caecum', still less when reduced to
bush-kill, the idea of 'pure nature ... without embodiment' seems far
from the human condition. The underlying question in all this consid-
eration of bodily existence, pain, humiliation and extinction, is whether
we are ultimately 'something else again'.

> One of the discoveries of 'modernist' poetry has been the technique
> of transposing the hopeless 'irritation of the jostled', 'the gross
> silence' of hired concealers', into the kind of rapid juxtapositions
> and violent lacunae that one finds in the third and fourth poems of
> *Hugh Selwyn Mauberley* – phrase callously jostling with phrase,
> implication merging into implication ('pli selon pli'), sententiae
> curtly abandoned. (*EC* pp. 94–5)

We see all of this in *Speech! Speech!* This juxtaposition of eyes in these vari-
ous contexts – Butler's 'wherever we turn our eyes' – is indeed 'callous',
perhaps especially when associated in the convenience of my expository
patterning here. Returning to the first Tanner Lecture, and the discussion
of Butler, we recall Hill quoting him on '"our ignorance, the imperfection
of our nature, our virtue and our condition in this world"' and immedi-
ately saying himself that these qualities 'are intrinsic to our creatureli-
ness'.[12] This 'creatureliness' is very bodily in the poem. The pain of the
image of Nzeogwu's eyes and the proctologist's examination are of a piece
in a way reminiscent of Swift. This 'jostling' – more than that, embattle-
ment – is part of the complexity of life, especially of 'POLITICS'. Are Fajuyi,
Nzeogwu, Okigbo heroes, 'living as they have to'? This phrase 'living as
they have to' is a running joke in *Speech! Speech!* But it has deep implica-
tions because it invites judgement between the contingent and the freely
chosen. In his essay 'Poetry as "Menace" and "Atonement"' Hill com-
pares the war poets Charles Sorley and Rupert Brooke. For Brooke the war
appeared as 'a sacrificial exploit', whereas for Sorley 'it is merely the con-
duct demanded of him (and others) by the turn of circumstances, where
non-compliance with this demand would have made life intolerable' (*LL*
p. 10). Like Fajuyi, Nzeogwu and Okigbo, Sorley was not an unconnected
monadic self but someone jostled by the actual circumstances he found

himself in. The self – 'this harp of nerves' (3) – has to exist with all that is 'not-self'. Hill uses the phrase 'not-self' in 'Poetry as "Menace" and "Atonement"' to illuminate the individual poet's relationship to language and to poetic form and structure: 'From the depths of the self we rise to a concurrence with that which is not-self' (*LL* p. 3). But we might here understand the phrase to encompass all kinds of external, contingent pressures, especially of politics. For Hill, *enduring* them is a particular kind of heroism ill-served by the notion of sacrifice.

It is here we can see Hill's fascination with Thomas Hobbes's *Leviathan*, which he calls, in his first Tanner Lecture, 'whatever else it is or is not, [is] a tragic elegy on the extinction of intrinsic value', and that 'Hobbes' despair, in *Leviathan*, arises from the extinction of personal identity'. To be protected from the depredations of the 'state of nature', which, as the late English Civil War had shown, consumes individual lives, the self must consign itself to the 'not-self' of the Leviathan state. But does this fatalism produced by our fear of Hobbes's 'state of nature' and our acquiescence to Leviathan annihilate, or relieve us of conscience?[13] There are twin but contradictory fears at work throughout *Speech! Speech!* One often comes in the guise of a scatty superstition that one could be found out, that there will be a reckoning. This can be heard at the opening of 10: 'From the beginning the question how to end / has been part of the act.' Then 11 begins 'Is MUST a true imperative of OUGHT?' and ends 'God / how I'd like to, if I could only, / shuffle off alive'. In 30:

> However you look at it you might
> fancy yourself saved by some careless genie
> numerate but illiterate

and ends with a smug, yet nervous triumph: 'What did I tell you – see – / they can't touch us.' The other fear is that *indeed* 'they can't touch us', nothing can touch us. There is no judgement and therefore no responsibility. We can discount 'ethics and such-like'. In 68 Justice appears as a profoundly ambiguous image. The section evokes aged former prisoners from the war with Japan whose whole subsequent lives have been discounted and 'shabbily unsorrowed'. Justice appears as a mighty ghost, impressive but perhaps impotent:

> Justice I transparent bale-fire of vanities:
> massive, shimmering I through incoherence.

'Bale-fire of the vanities' nods towards the contemporary satirist Tom Wolfe,[14] but the ancient term 'bale-fire' carries many of the same connotations as its more familiar synonym. Is it a *feu de joie*, a beacon, a pyre, or

– and this is the distinctiveness of the word – the ravening flames of evil, as 'bale' specifically suggests? The image is so nearly beautiful, but its rhythm is deliberately hobbled by the speech-marks, and it is just as nearly terrible – baleful indeed. Whichever – or both – it is glimpsed through incoherence, the babble of an ever-more garrulous culture which threatens to drown all order of sense and significance. This is the condition that the poem is always enacting and always combating. To do so it cannot maintain 'the sublime in the old sense' but must soil itself, and – *nasum in ano* – rub our noses in it. To maintain a distinctive voice, sometimes by jabbing the reader with diacritics to be sure we *hear* it right, is the great struggle of the poem. Moreover, to achieve such a voice is to resist Hobbes's despair and to maintain an ethical responsibility, albeit one that is never transcendent but always beset by our creaturely being. Which is why this work is rough, crude, 'ugly'. Beauty is indeed difficult.

9 'Here and there I pull a flower': *The Orchards of Syon* (2002)

The Orchards of Syon completes a tentative trilogy begun with *The Triumph of Love* and continued with *Speech! Speech!* 'Tentative' because all three-part sequences are bound to refer to the model of Dante's *La Divina Commedia*, as, I shall show, Hill's can be seen to do, and that is a model haunted by hubris. Hill's *commedia* is fraught with the anxiety, anger, doubt, self-doubt and self-flagellation that besets Dante, and is similarly bold in its historical and referential reach. But part of its comedy lies in parody and self-mockery, a recurrent wariness of pretension and the pratfall: '*La vida es sueño?* I ought / to read it, before they say I haven't' (*Syon* XV).

It is because of this strongly reflexive and parodic element that I think another work written in three 'partitions', Robert Burton's *The Anatomy of Melancholy*,[1] might also be recognised as conveying itself into Hill's trilogy. There is some warrant for this in Hill's discussion of Burton in his essay 'Keeping to the Middle Way', published in *The Times Literary Supplement* in December 1994 and reprinted in *Style and Faith* (2003), but I do not think that the suggestion relies upon it. If there is one characteristic above all others that marks off *The Triumph*, *Speech!* and *Syon* it is the comparative loquacity, even garrulity, of the style. There is a talkative, often cascading quality to the manner. This is most explicit in *Speech! Speech!* where the sycophantic urging of the title is torrentially answered. But the longer sections of *The Triumph*, and the strophes of the twenty-four-line poems of *Syon*, affect what Burton, writing of his own work, calls an 'extemporanean style' (Everyman p. 26). Here is an instance:

> We are – what, all of us? – near death. So wave
> me your solution. *Cupio dissolvi,*
> Saul's vital near-death experience more
> sandblasted than lasered. *Beam*
> *us up, Asrael.* High talk, dissolution
> expansive, all pervasive; here it coils
> back into density: dark angel, fused,

rubberoid, shrunk, foetal, as though raked
from Zeppelin ashes. Immortal
Death, lovely suppliant!
Orphée I saw six times in the one week.
(IV)

The jotted, associational character of these lines, together with the
unfilled syntax, freely various line-lengths and breaks, and scattered allu-
sions, all contribute to the sense of the poet's extemporising. It is not so
far from the manner of a poet whom most of Hill's readers must have
been surprised to see acknowledged in the *Paris Review* interview of
2000,[2] and in *Syon* XXXVII and XLV, Frank O'Hara. This is from
O'Hara's 'Avenue A':

We hardly ever see the moon any more
                              so no wonder
    it's so beautiful when we look up suddenly
and there it is gliding broken-faced over the bridges
brilliantly coursing, soft, and a cool wind fans
        your hair over your forehead and your memories
            of Red Grooms' locomotive landscape
I want some bourbon/you want some oranges/I love the leather
        jacket Norman gave me
                        and the corduroy coat David
    gave you, it is more mysterious than spring, the El Greco
heavens breaking open and then reassembling like lions
                        in a vast tragic veldt
    that is far from our small selves and our temporally united
passions in the cathedral of Januaries[.][3]

In his mock-criticism of his own style Burton describes it thus:

And for those other faults of barbarism, Doric dialect, extempo-
ranean style, tautologies, apish imitation, a rhapsody of rags gath-
ered from several dung-hills, excrements of authors, toys and
fopperies confusedly tumbled out, without art, invention, judge-
ment, wit, learning, harsh, rude, phantastical, absurd, insolent,
indiscreet, ill-composed, indigested, vain, scurrile, idle, dull, and
dry; I confess all ('tis partly affected), thou canst not think worse
of me than I do myself. (Everyman p. 26)

A critique of Hill's style in *Syon* – mock or otherwise – might identify
many of these elements. 'Doric' colloquialisms intensify that ear for
cliché long familiar in his work: 'knackered' (IX), 'It's safe bet' (XI), 'I

should be so lucky' (XXIII), 'bloody silly' (XXV), 'Be serious' (XXXIX); 'Up against' (XLII), 'Say what you will' (XLIII) often appear at the outset of poems. There are Americanisms: 'dooryard', 'backlot' (XXIX) 'intersection' (XXXV). Groaning puns: 'it is more than age he girns for' (IX), BRUCE L. OSIS and T. B. D. KLINING' (XXXIX), 'Outage not / outrage' (XXIX). Subversive wordplay: 'Eat whose heart out?' (XXV), 'Strophe after strophe / ever more catastrophic. Did I say / strophe? I meant salvo, sorry' (X), 'collages of dashed peace' (XII), 'I desire so not to deny desire's / intransigence' (LV). Vocabularies are mixed in phrases like 'the contra-Faustian heist' (I). Rare and dialect words are prominent: 'swaling Hodder' (XXXII), 'dibble-holes' (LXIX), 'dwale' (LXVIII), 'reddle' (XXIII), 'selvage' (XLIX), and Gerard Manley Hopkins's 'pash' (XLVI),[4] along with heavily Latinate items such as 'eximious' (LXIV), 'penumbrate' (IX). Coinages such as 'chobbles', (XVIII) 'gurney' as a verb (II), 'spinnrad' (XXXVI). And there are macaronic moments: '*enceinte* with sorrow' (IV), 'riding that *vague*' (V), after Burton's 'this my *Macaronicon*' (p. 25). Among the 'rhapsody of rags gathered from several dung-hills, excrements of authors' might be counted all the allusions from Dante to the Ealing comedy *Passport to Pimlico* by way of Cocteau, Matthew Boulton and Havergal Brian. That in all this we see 'fopperies confusedly tumbled out, without art, invention, judgement' is the kind of verdict familiarly delivered by Hill's reviewers. Burton's self-defence includes the pre-emptive apology: 'thou canst not think worse of me than I do myself', and this is a stratagem Hill also employs. Sometimes its irony is palpable and contemptuously aimed, as in that 'I ought / to read it before they say I haven't'. Elsewhere the confession is pitched more introspectively:

> I'm
> myself close to the inarticulate. Commonplace
> muddledom I grant, extraordinary
> common goodness being its twin.
>
> (LXIII)

Also, in LXIX, we read 'conglomerate roots / of words. I wish I could say more.' That last sentence is an instance of the re-presentation of a cliché 'rinsed' (as Christopher Ricks long since and memorably described it)[5] of its fingered grime so that it loses all trace of the formulaic mumble or dismissive shrug to become the simple utterance of stricken inadequacy.

But, as with Burton, how seriously are we take these admissions? Clearly there is a rebarbative, even a cussed, element in both authors which does not for a moment accept the charges. These are *faux* apologies. Yet Hill has always been vexed by words, by how glutinous their conglomerations can become and the muddle they can produce. Now, especially in *The Orchards of Syon* with its frequently more directly personal address, there is a new inflection to this anxiety.

I think this can also be described through the association with *The Anatomy of Melancholy* for to some extent that title also describes Hill's purpose here. Burton styles himself 'Democritus Junior' after the pre-Socratic philosopher Democritus, a ploy of persona of a kind Hill often uses, and says of Democritus's own Anatomy that its subject 'was melancholy and madness', and its intent that 'he might better cure it in himself, and by his writings and observations teach others how to prevent and avoid it' (p. 20). He himself – 'Democritus Junior' – writes 'of melancholy, by being busy to avoid melancholy': '*stultus labor est ineptiarum*, to be busy in toys is to small purpose, yet hear that divine Seneca, better *aliud agere quam nihil*, better do to no end than nothing'. Burton insists upon his subject, of melancholy as being 'the character of mortality' (p. 143). Later, in 'Democritus Junior's' preface, he reproves one who has been mocking 'an old man, that by reason of his age was a little fond', in these terms: 'What madness ghosts this old man? But, What madness ghosts us all? For we are *ad unum omnes*, all mad … say it of us all, *semper pueri*, young and old, all dote …' Hill begins XLII:

> Up against ageing and dying I stand bemused
> by labours of flight: a low-geared heron
> retiring to its pool, the shapes that gulls
> beat and tack[.]

In this staggeringly beautiful descriptive sequence he is transfixed in turn by a crow, small birds, a kestrel and moths, then on to 'murmurings of the Kaddish'. Here, as in many of the progresses in these poems, he might be said to 'dote', that is 'to be silly, deranged, or out of one's wits; to act or talk foolishly or stupidly' (*OED*). In present use the word is almost always associated with senescence, 'dotage' – and this too is a recurrent reference, and one of the fears that haunts the book. His book is busy enough in its syntactical varieties, in its tessellation of images and references, but might it not amount to *stultus labor*, stultifying labour, mere occupation, only better than nothing? The *OED* cites the 1611 Bible: 'doting about questions and strifes of wordes', for which, it states, Tyndale translated 'wasteth his braynes'.

> I desire so not to deny desire's
> intransigence. To you I stand
> answerable. Correction: must once have stood.
> What's this thing, like a clown's eyebrow-brush?
> O my lady, it is the fool's confession,
> weeping greasepaint, all paint and rhetoric.
>
> (LV)

'Questions and strifes of wordes' have always been at the centre of Hill's work in both verse and prose. The rampant soliloquies and addresses to persons known and unknown of the trilogy, with their murmurings, sudden hectorings, abrupt questions, truculent and apologetic by turns, often interrupted by noises off, drives fascinatingly near the obsessional quality of those bemused monologists sometimes encountered on the top deck of a bus. He risks that it might very well be 'the fool's confession'.

In his essay 'Keeping to the Middle Way', Hill compares the ostensible manner of Burton's *Anatomy* with more austere seventeenth-century strictures on the proper manners of writing and speech. He adduces John Donne's ordinance that since 'God speaks to us in *oratione stricta*, in limited, in a diligent form: Let us [not] speak to him *in oratione soluta*' [unrestrainedly] (*SF* p. 61). By this standard, writes Hill, or by that of Hobbes with his 'laconic scorn, dismissive of logorrhoea', 'Burton is likely to appear "loose"'. He draws attention to how the word *stultus* has 'clearly snagged [Burton's] mind', and that he 'could perhaps be said to have invented, to suit his own sense of decorum (which is strong), an English form of *stultiloquium* (= a foolish babbling) ... several years before "stultiloquy" appeared in English usage', and then pejoratively in Jeremy Taylor's dismissal of 'meer Stultiloquy, or talking like a foole', in 1653 (*SF* p. 62). The forces ranged against a manner of writing such as Burton's are intimidating. Who can sustain themselves against the charge of 'talking like a foole'? Moreover Hill puts in play another formidable phrase, this one drawn from Cornwallis on Seneca (1601), writing of 'the true discourse of the minde', a phrase close to Hobbes in *Leviathan* when laying down a definition of 'the Discourse of the Mind' (*SF* p. 61). Surely stultiloquy has no part in such a discourse, still less the kindred quality which Burton owns up to of being a dabbler: 'I am but a smatterer, I confess, a stranger, here and there I pull a flower' (p. 33). However, Hill claims 'the nature of the true discourse of the mind ... to be the central issue of *The Anatomy of Melancholy*', and goes on to argue how Burton's method provides a truer anatomy of that discourse.

A defence of *The Orchards of Syon* would need to identify, even anatomise, 'the nature of the true discourse of the mind', even though

it is a discourse that risks stultiloquy. The book dotes upon memory. In
The Triumph of Love memory was very much a public concern about his-
torical forgetting, and it is in *Syon* too, but here it is more particular in
that the book presents the texture of a particular mind at different levels
of its consciousness.

'The man / is old' (IX), and as the greater part of life becomes
memory so is he the more and more transfixed by it.

> Memory is its own vision, a gift of sight,
> from which thought step aside, and frequently,
> into the present, where we have possession
> more and more denied us.
>
> (LIV)

As the present shrinks, so does remembering become the discourse of
the mind. But what is the nature of remembering? Does it, for instance,
have a different substance from that of dreaming? If life is now over-
whelmingly memory, and the character of memory and dream in the
mind are indistinguishable, then is life a dream? The title of Calderón's
play *La vida es sueño* – 'life is a dream' – occurs in the first poem and is
a running reference thereafter. On one level it is a running joke: 'Has it
ever been staged / seriously outside Spain' (I), 'I ought / to read it
before they say I haven't' (XV), 'see, I remembered! (XXV). But under
this is the anxiety of annihilation, the fear that what happened, what mat-
tered, what hurt and what was joyful, exists now only in the 'shadow-
play' of memory, that erratic, grainy and dissolving palimpsest – and
therefore never mattered.

> So much
> of time is rubble. Under the sky's
> great clearances, not oúr time only.
>
> (V)

The book's mental states are on this shifting margin between the present
and the variously remembered past, but also in the space adjacent to death.

This is the significance of the recurrent references to Cocteau's film
Orphée. The work has appeared in *The Triumph of Love* (CXXVIII) where
he evokes the unsettling and hypnotically narcissistic world of the film in
which the poet Orpheus, the sinisterly beautiful Princess of Death, and
other characters move between life and death:

> Dipping their (rubber-sheathed) hands to the wrist
> in vats of quicksilver, they were absorbed
> by bedroom-mirrors through which the interchange
> of life with death began and ended.

In *Syon* poem IV begins 'We are – what, all of us? – near death.' Now there is a sensual enthralment to all this. 'Immortal / Death, lovely suppliant! / *Orphée* I saw six times in the one week', embodied in Maria Casarès's sable eroticism – but one note in the sequence's sexual *leitmotif* – is absorbed with a nearly adolescent fervour. The compulsion here is also bound up with a fascinated knowingness about how the film-maker contrives his effects. In *The Triumph* he dwells on how Cocteau 'moved angles, elevations, to revitalize / young gay men mercurial', and in *Syon*:

> I understand Hell's surreal ruins to be
> those of the blitzed Académie de St Cyr,
> with wind machines off camera[.]
>
> (IV)

The film-buff's 'how do they do that?' curiosity is however shadowed by the ironies of artifice – here in particular the use of the military academy destroyed in the war as the film-set for this fable – but more generally the jolt some inventions can give to appearance as when, in *The Triumph*, he describes how a First World War infantry advance 'stops dead: machine-guns do the work / of trick photography' (*TL* CXXVIII). This inversion is more arresting than the 'life imitating art' cliché could encompass, and points to Hill's deep ambivalence about artifice. It is vital and admired but also suspected as a heartless lust for effect. Hill's clear fascination with the cinema is as much marked by this preoccupation as is his suspicion of verse: 'Begin with golden curtains ... Exit – / through heavy resistant side-doors – in a daze' (*Syon* XI).

So this dwelling or doting upon the 'interchange of life with death' is reflexive even to the point of parody. But just as being shot does 'the work of trick photography', so this knowingness brings the implacable knowledge of death. We are – yes, all of us – near death, but '*Du calme* counsels the Princess', familiar with the effect of death:

> Her tragic shadow – pulled
> through – down and across – is swept
> off the blank end wall.
>
> (IV)

Is death a trick of the light, just as life is but a trick of memory? But the elegant resignation of Cocteau's Princess of Death is not so easy to achieve in life. Just as Hill's wry response to Coleridge's claim that 'poets leap over death' is 'did anyone see him do it and live?' (*Syon* XXXVI), so oblivion is not infinitely desirable: 'Concentrate / in face of oblivion. *Ce n'est pas drôle*' (*Syon* LXVIII). It's no joke, as even the Princess admits, for the self cannot remain calm:

> Whose is the voice, faint, injured and ghostly,
> trapped in this cell phone, if it is not mine?
> Some voices ride easily the current. Some
> lives get away with murder any road.
> How slowly – *without discord* – all hurls to oblivion.
>
> (XXX)

The pun on 'cell' is characteristic, but what appears characteristic is the acknowledgement of who is speaking. Voice recognition has always been an issue and a game in reading Hill. This later work has certainly doffed the personae of earlier work (whether or not those were 'masks'). As I've remarked already it has a more 'extemporanean' aspect, more in the character of a journal. In the same *Paris Review* interview Hill revises his long-held view of 'impersonality' in poetry as understood from Eliot's essay 'Tradition and the Individual Talent'.[6] It may not be too much to say that the voice has long been trapped in the cell of the poem.

But the reality of death and the evanescence of memory press fictiveness to its limit. As all 'hurls to oblivion' what particles might adhere? 'if this / is the home-straight, where is my fixed home?' (XXX). We can catch one thing that adheres in those last lines of this poem: 'Some / lives get away with murder any road.' There's a deliberate blunt disgruntlement made up of the cliché 'get away with murder' and the English Midlands locution of 'any road' instead of the more refined and received 'anyway'. Notable too is the move from 'voices' to 'lives', a shift accentuated by the abrupt line-break. In the familiar phrase it is usually 'some folk' or 'some people get away with murder'. 'Lives' is an intensification, for whereas 'voice' is bound to be to some extent a synecdoche for the whole person, 'life' involves the span of the whole being and emphasises that span, whereas 'people' or 'folk' might only imply a single, or maybe several instances, even if the qualification of 'usually' is commonly understood in this phrase. The certain implication the phrase carries is 'some get away', but not me: *I* am held to account. What cannot be shaken off, no matter how insubstantial and thus inconsequential life can seem to become, is the notion of justice.

The next few poems worry at justice and judgement. In XXXI we are in the inferno with 'Dante's trope / of Justice', and 'the incorrigible / nature of judgement'. In XXXIII the poet regrets indifference,

> As if
> no one's of account, or takes, or gives, account
> beyond some timeless exigence, the fall
> of determined sparrows

but glimpses at the end 'a clear verdict from the scales'. Lives do not dissolve painlessly into the inscrutable distance of Providence (how sardonically Hill mocks Hamlet's blandness in that comic belittling pun on '*determined* sparrows'). The most commonplace contemplation will bring live pain, as in LXVI where the poet seems to be standing before his parents' grave:

> I can torment myself
> with simple gratitude, municipal
> salvias in the restyled garden of rest
> staring my thoughts back.

There is an obstinate, unkillable sense of what is due, of the importance of making a proper account of the uncounted. Such pains of omission and commission, and the ethical demand, mean that this is never a dream: *ce n'est pas drôle.*

But 'the incorrigible nature of judgement' can be experienced as consuming the self and the world with its implacability. In the sequence LVII, LVIII and LIX, Hill revolts against its implications:

> Reading Dante in a mood of angry dislike
> for my fellow sufferers and for myself
> that I dislike them.
>
> (LVII)

'The words of justice … make a sudden / *psst psst* like farrier's hot iron on horn.' Here the rigours of judgement are felt as inimical and even paradoxical. In the next poem he chafes at recognising how his mind is fixated on the Fall and *eternal* damnation figured in the manner of the Massachusetts revivalist preacher Jonathan Edwards's vision of human beings held over the fiery pit like spiders above hot coals:

> in this one-off temerity, arachnidous,
> abseiling into a pit, the pit a void,
> a black hole, a galaxy in denial.
>
> (LVIII)

LIX begins:

> Never cared much for righteous WICLIF. His
> *heavenly country* meant the Kingdom of Heaven.
> Chosen by and for the elect.

The truncated syntax of these throwaway dismissals mimics the peremptoriness of the self-assured elect. Mockery of how incommensurable are eternal damnation foretold and an individual life as lived, has already been articulated, more comically, in XI. Here the poem leaps from an evocation of the comeuppance Ealing film comedies reserve for the 'impudent' and 'feckless' ('Watch them frogmarched off') to closure as envisaged in Isaac Watts's desperately stern *The Day of Judgement*: 'dire codicil / to human mood and thought'. If absence of accountability is unacceptable so too is the ruthlessness of implacable judgement. The latter is also fuelled by different levels of paranoia. One might be arraigned for real culpability but also frogmarched off for some literary peccadillo: 'I ought to read it before they say I haven't.' But then there is the anxiety of 'the person / always on call, always answerable, / a witness that can barely be suppressed' (XV). 'They' are never far from Hill's imaginings. Perhaps part of his fascination with Cocteau's *Orphée* lies in the anonymous judges whose bureaucratic mien and procedures seem in no way formidable, indeed verge on self-parody, but in fact hold everything, including death herself, in thrall.

To reject both indifference and statutory damnation is to reject two certainties and thus two simplifications. Redemption, by which can be meant being redeemed from damnation or from meaninglessness, is never clearly seen:

> Redemption
> is self-redemption and entails crawling
> to the next angle of vision.
> Press the right word, the scenes change.
> (XXXIV)

Life in the world is perpetually in flux and uncertainty. Poem XLVII beginning '*In Terra Pax*', pictures the earth as a war-zone, blasted, disinhabited, or as the wrecked hive-cities of Max Ernst's painting 'Europe After the Rain', or the denatured, smeared impasto of an Anselm Kiefer canvas. The way through to resolution and peace cannot be seen from on high but is a journey of inches:

> Come down from your high
> thrones of question, good doctors of wisdom.
> Now Í am at ground level and must grope,
> whereas the blinded archangel stands clear
> on his chance tottering ledge.

Yet the poem does not give up on *in terra pax*. In the last two lines it is

> dark in itself but sighted, as dead stars
> that overlook us with a splittering light.

It is the ultimate seriousness of the world that demands this 'crawling', but also there is the 'splittering light' – which splinters and splits – that shows us something other. Moreover this vision is in, and of, the sensuously apprehended world. Both the doctrines of dream and condemnation reject the world, but in *The Orchards of Syon* the physical world of our mortality is always before us whether it is as solid as 'shippens / built of random masonry' (LIX), as evanescent as 'Dame Rainbow' (LXXII), as handsome as 'the stooped pear-tree [which] honours with its shade' (LIX), or as ugly as the heart exposed on an operating table which 'leaps fattily, apes a sexual motion / as if copulating with itself' (LX). These are 'mortal beauty' and through them are vouchsafed moments of transfiguration. In the continuance of the poem beginning with Wiclif we read, surely in a voice where the I is least hedged round:

> All along, I'm labouring to try out
> a numen that endures, exactly placed:
> some upper valley in the high fell country
> where millstone grit juts against limestone;
>   (LIX)

and there follows a series of humble, acutely realised images culminating in the 'the stooped pear-tree'. It is numena like these that form the Orchards of Syon.

> Tell me, is this the way
> to the Orchards of Syon
> where I left you thinking I would return?
>   (I)

'Syon' – a less militant spelling of 'Zion' – is the promised land, and its orchards part of medieval visionary imagination. Here it is the sensuousness of the phrase that matters along with the redolence of blossoming beauty and Eden. In the poem it has several metonyms: 'Goldengrove', the rainbow, Eden itself, and it is associated too with music. Syon is not a time or place but a mental vision. At one specific moment Hill yearns briefly to locate it in his childhood home:

> And here – and there too – I
> wish greatly to believe: that Bromsgrove
> was, and is, Goldengrove; that the Orchards
> of Syon stand as I once glimpsed them.
> But there we are: the heartland remains
> heartless – that's the strange beauty of it.
>   (XXXVIII)

Nonetheless, though Syon is numinous, its lineaments are emphatically of the physical world, 'uncannily of the earth'. This appearance, in XIII, shows several of its significances:

> Patchy weather, quick
> showers gusting the fields like clouds of lime.
> You thought us held by favours: see above.
> Such are the starts of memory, abrupt
> blessing slid from confusion. Await
> new-fangled light, the slate roofs briefly
> caught in scale-nets of silver, then
> sheened with thin oils. These signals
> I take as apprehension, new-aligned
> poetry with truth, and Syon's Orchards
> uncannily of the earth.

Syon is startling in its appearances, a neuronal flash like 'the starts of memory'. The detailed beauty and transitoriness of light is also part of it, and being caught by such moments is, as the poem has said at its beginning, a blessing. Commonly the sights of Syon are 'light-endowed' (XII), as in the changes in the colour of a fell-side 'through brimming heat-haze' (XIV); the sun 'bringing on strongly now each flame-recognizance' (XXIV); the 'intermittent / cloud-shadow across roofs' in the Bromsgrove poem (XXXVIII); 'even in winter, / the sun digs silver out of the evergreen' for Syon's 'tenebrous thresholds / of illumination' (LIV). But it is the intermittence and elusiveness of light as well as its furnishing glory that is foregrounded. In this regard 'shuttery' light is like the 'shutter / play among words, befitting / a pact with light' (I). Catching these apprehensions through the labour of precise description within the phantasm of words identifies poetry with truth.

Another notable characteristic of these descriptions is how humble are the things noticed. We have seen this before in 'each separate bead / of drizzle at its own thorn-tip' in LIII of *The Triumph of Love*, and 'the potato vine in its places / of lowly flowering' in *TL* LVIII. Here such modest flowers are again drawn into admiring attention: 'How beautiful the world unrecognized / through most of seventy years ... The hawthorn all the more fulfilling its beauty' (V). This 'world unrecognized' includes 'many-headed the field / rose, dog rose, tossing in bright squalls' (XII); 'the despised / ragwort, luminous, standing out, / stereoscopically, across twenty yards' (XX); 'The hellebore, the Christmas rose, is crowned king' (XXVII) (the hellebore also appears in *TL* VI). Sometimes, as with the 'broad verges' and 'spare garden plots with pear and apple / or with wild damson' (LV) we sense this to be the closely felt micro-habitation of childhood like the bower of ferns in '*The Landscape / of Childhood*' in XXXVIII:

> Did we shield then, believe it, hope to die,
> those all-marvelling, unrehearsed
> hours, where goldcrests and the great ferns were,
> *Osmunda regalis*, bowing us in and down,
> both royal and nesh?

This is the world of the 'Child's play' in 'the crypt of roots | and endings' in *Mercian Hymns* (IV), and that modest, extraordinary realm of the 'self-desolating child'. In *Syon* the 'doomed childhood' of III might be personal pain – 'self-inflicted / wounds of morose delectation' – but also anticipates the eventuality of damnation: 'How is this life adjudged / derelict, a stress-bearer since Eden?' Altogether they have a consoling, even healing quality, and indeed, other obscure plants that are the herbalist's 'simples' also figure: woundwort (VIII and XIX), haemony (IX), centaury (XIV), horehound (LVI). The Orchards of Syon with the lustrous bounty of their 'heavy-bearing trees bowed towards Fall' (XXII), 'sway-backed with pear and apple, / the plum, in spring and autumn resplendent' (LXX), are a counterweight to damnation and the Fall. To some extent they lean against the devastated orchards, ravaged Eden:

> Orchards of the *bocage*, June through October,
> sloughed odours of death from tracked armour
> gone multiflame. Decaying glider-fabric,
> knicker-silk parachutes, umbelliferae,
> littering the hedgerows, the barn-rubble,
> and splintered crofts.
>
> (XLIV)

This is 'the human midden' of warfare, (the number of the section alluding to Normandy '44), 'despoiler of Goldengrove / and Syon's Orchards' (LX).

What the whole work seeks to identify in the world as we know it is some opening from this world, something that transfigures it. This is the common theme of the book's three epigraphs. The sentences from Thomas Bradwardine's *De Causa Dei* seek it:

> It seemed that I saw, though at a distance, within the image or form
> of Truth (this being wholly transparent), God's grace already pre-
> sent in time as in nature, before any good works existed.

In a more secular mode, in D. H. Lawrence's *The Rainbow* Tom Brangwen breaks off from the drunken exhilaration of Anna and Will's wedding party to a wholly different exaltation:

> The night was flashing with stars. Sirius blazed like a signal at the
> side of the hill. Orion, stately and magnificent, was sloping along
> … 'It's a fine night,' said Tom.

And a third, Thomas Traherne, in his *Centuries of Meditations*: 'Everything was at rest, free, and immortal.' *The Orchards of Syon* does not, any more than any of Hill's previous books, show a world 'at rest, free, and immortal', or the certain radiance of God's grace spreading everywhere, but the fleeting rainbow can appear in even the most unexpected of moments and places:

> Pub car-park puddles, radiant cauls of oil.
> When all else fails, the great rainbow, as Bert
> Lawrence saw it or summoned it.
>   (XLVIII)

The rainbow, like the fragile orchards and the departing Goldengrove, is an image of transcendent beauty that is also an emblem of mutability, and, moreover, delusion. Thus such apprehensions might be seen to laugh back, but despite this they still lodge obstinately in the poet's mind.

This is why Gerard Manley Hopkins is so prominent a presence in the work. His elegy for summer, 'Margaret are you grieving / Over Goldengrove unleaving', is of course a major leitmotif ('Goldengrove' also draws upon Jeremy Taylor's Welsh retreat during the Civil War) and is thus part of the work's 'hermeneutics of autumn' (XXIV). He is a spirit too of one of the work's most important places, the fell and river country of the Hodder Valley in north Lancashire. Some of Hill's most magnificent descriptions are of this landscape. For instance, poem XX begins 'Two nights' and three days' rain, with the Hodder / well up, over its alder roots', and, after pausing over that 'despised ragwort', follows the river 'downstream from this Quaker outcrop' to Hopkins's Stonyhurst whose strange incongruity of northern fustian and continental exoticism is precisely notated in the conjunctions 'Loyola and English weather' and 'stone, *pelouse*'. But theologically the company of Hopkins has to do with the problem of 'mortal beauty'. 'Mortal beauty is alienation; or not, / as I see it' (XX). Just as Hopkins could not wholly accede to orthodoxy and school his eyes away from the intense 'thisness', *haeccitas* – in his own invented term, 'inscape' – of the physical world, but sought the divine within it, so Hill's own apprehensions of the individuated particularities of nature – 'the

despised / ragwort, luminous, standing out' (XX) – form his own version
of inscape which is an escape from dull determination. One of Hopkins's
later appearances follows the uplifting rainbow in XLIX: 'Hopkins, who
was self- / belaboured, crushed, cried out being uplifted', then:

> Imagine your own way
> out of necessity; imagine
> no need to do this. Good story, bad
> ending, if narrative is the element
> that so overreaches. Providence
> used to be worked-in, somewhere. I, at best,
> conjecture divination. The rainbow's
> appearance covenants with reality.
>
> (XLIX)

Note the punning phrase 'Imagine your own way / out of necessity'.
Individuation is consonant with individual resistance against Necessity.
Matter of factly, there is no other option.

Just how important individuation is here can be glimpsed in yet
another figure in the book, the German word *Atemwende*. The word
appears six times in two clusters and in sequences of lines that are par-
ticularly sombre. The first cluster – XXVIII, XXXI, XXXII and XXXVI –
is notably wintry. The second – LI and LII – concentrates upon word-
play, including some heavyweight deadpan punning on foreign words:
'Ostracizm's a small foothill town / in the Carpathians that retires at
dusk' (LI); 'Cicatrice is no dead insect' (LII). The prominence of word-
ing here is important because at each appearance of *Atemwende* the work
worries at its translation into English: '*atem-* / *wende*, breath-hitch say'
(XXVIII); *Atemwende*: / catch-breath, breath-ply' (XXXI); '*Atemwende*,
/ breath-fetch' (XXXII); '*Atemwende*, turn / of breath' (XXXVI); 'You
could render / *atemwende* as breath-glitch' (LI); and in LII we have
'each moment's / epiphany's much like a betrayal / of held breath'. Cold
catches the breath, an involuntary reflex like the cold-tears that make
'flowerets, faceted clusters, out of clear brights' such as headlights and
signal gantries (XXX). It is a moment of arrest, breath taken away in an
astonishment that breaks up the ordinary. It is too of course the threat
or shock of death. XXVIII, where *Atemwende* appears first, begins:

> Wintry swamp-thickets, brush-heaps of burnt light.
> The sky cast-iron, livid with unshed snow.
> I cannot say what it is that best
> survives these desolations. Something does,
> unlovely; indomitable as the mink.

It is a vision of despair, a dull, lifeless landscape with the 'brush-heaps' bled of any autumnal lustre. Sardonically it is then likened to the annihilation of close-down in black-and-white television. In this extremity

> Nothing prepares us
> for such fidelity of observation,
> I would observe. Nothing to be struck out
> of like finalities. *Atemwende*,
> CELAN almost at last gasp, *atem-*
> *wende*, breath-hitch, say;

Paul Celan's volume of poems *Atemwende* includes a poem called 'Ein Dröhnen'. This is Michael Hamburger's translation:

> A RUMBLING: truth
> itself has appeared
> among humankind
> in the very thick of their
> flurrying metaphors.[7]

Nothing is more individually felt than the physical breath. Nothing more astounding than its unexpected interruptions, catches, gasps, hitches, fetches, glitches. Breath is also the stuff of language but it is not its regularity in voluble discourse, 'the very thick of ... / flurrying metaphors', that matters most in *The Orchards of Syon*, but these desperate but wondrous punctuations, the 'starts of memory', the certain slants of light, untranslatable *Atemwende* that seize the poet and his readers. Hill has referred to Pound's 'Beauty is a brief gasp between one cliché and another'[8] and these are some of those 'brief gasps'. This work does not have sequence and coherence, and finally the trilogy cannot be seen as having destination in the Dantean sense. Hill sees no organised Paradise, but amid the flurry of the determined extempore, surrounded by and in stultiloquy, stands not stultified but amazed before what he has made into his emblem. Vision does not lose out 'to wandering speculation' (XXIX), but, 'as apprehension, new-aligned / poetry with truth', (XIII), is put before us at the end:

> .Here are the Orchards of Syon, neither wisdom
> nor illusion of wisdom, not
> compensation, not recompense: the Orchards
> of Syon whatever harvests we bring them.
>   (LXXII)

10 'In wintry solstice like the shorten'd light': Scenes from Comus (2005)

> Erewhile of music, and ethereal mirth,
> Wherewith the stage of air and earth did ring,
> And joyous news of heavenly infant's birth,
> My muse with angels did divide to sing;
> But headlong joy is ever on the wing,
>   In wintry solstice like the shorten'd light
> Soon swallowed up in dark and long out-living night.

This is the first stanza of John Milton's 'The Passion', a poem he probably began and abandoned in 1630 (*Complete Shorter Poems* p. 119).[1] The penultimate line, as '*In Wintry solstice like the shorten'd light*', recurs in Geoffrey Hill's *Scenes from Comus*, including in the very last lines of the work. The whole three-part sequence is timed close to this solstice, poised on the edge of 'dark and long out-living night': 'over your / left shoulder or mine | absolute night comes / high-stalking after us' (2.80).[2] Milton's lines also point to another major preoccupation of Hill's poem, music. As Milton turns from the exultation of his preceding poem, 'On the Morning of Christ's Nativity', to the nadir of Christ's death, it seems that music as well as joy is annihilated. In fact the next stanza begins 'For now to sorrow must I tune my song, / And set my harp to notes of saddest woe', so it seems that he can fashion a different kind of music. In the event he could not for the work was laid aside after eight stanzas: '*The subject the author finding to be above the years he had when he wrote it, and nothing satisfied with what was begun, left it unfinished*' (*CSP* p. 122). Hill keeps his own music going towards 'long out-living night' when that of the young Milton fails, but his concern is not only with the endurance of his verse, here metaphorically cast as 'music'. Working across the frame of reference of Milton's 'Comus', 'A Masque presented at Ludlow Castle, 1634', (*CSP* pp. 168–229) Hill is thinking about music itself, and sounding its relation to, and difference from, words. Set before death, what is their substance?

Scenes from Comus is first an occasional poem, written 'for Hugh Wood on his 70th Birthday'. Wood, who composed his own *Scenes from*

Comus for soprano, tenor and orchestra between 1962 and 1965, is Hill's contemporary to the year and month, so the occasion can be seen to be doubled to take in Hill's own seventieth birthday. Indeed occasion is a central feature of Milton's masque since it was written with the composer Henry Lawes to celebrate the appointment in 1631 of the Earl of Bridgewater as President of the Council of Wales and Lord Lieutenant of Wales and the counties on the Welsh border. Milton's occasion is far more ostensibly public, indeed political, as the hazardous allegorical journey of the Lady and her two brothers through 'the perplexed paths of this drear wood', a strange western land under the mythological sway of Neptune and his half-human 'blue-haired deities', is meant to imply the uncertainties attending the Earl and his family as he wields his 'new-entrusted sceptre' in the Welsh Marches. As we shall see, these political resonances find their way into Hill's poem, but initially it is the more personal associations of the setting sun and of the masque's first performance on 29 September 1634 which is Michaelmas, the quarter-day prior to the winter solstice, that draw attention. The sun – 'that supreme / engine' (2.62) – and its varying shades – 'light's pyromania' (2.71) – are omnipresent. The poem is also 'set' narratively in Reykjavik where the Icelandic days of the closing year are yet shorter and whose Atlantic vistas evoke Milton's 'great Oceanus' and 'earth-shaking Neptune's mace' more proximately. Wave-beat, incorrigible, implacable, 'the sea's mood', its colours and shapes, 'greenish first, then mustard-yellow, / then chevroned, then broken up' (3.1), break recurrently through the poem, 'the sea guffawing off reefs' (1.4), 'the winter sea, / the *stormy Hebrides*', 'the breakers there / pile with such force you feel their breath expelled / in hearing it' (3.18). It is to this that 'we compose our daft music / of comprehension' (1.4). This is the greater context for the birthday occasion when, with dark jocularity, 'senna's called on more than single malt', and Hill, in darkly mischievous party mood, invites Wood 'Let's go to ground around the grinning cake' (1.3).

Occasion, ceremony and celebration draws us to consider the form of the masque with a view to discovering how Hill is using it. Of course all poems, however casually they propose themselves, are 'occasions' by virtue of the deliberation of their setting forth. Hill however has so frequently set his work forth within a prominently ceremonial framework, often drawn from musical forms: 'Requiem for the Plantagenet Kings', 'Canticle for Good Friday', 'Funeral Music ', *Mercian Hymns*, 'Two Chorale Preludes', *The Triumph of Love* among them. The Renaissance masque was a stylised courtly or aristocratic entertainment combining spectacle, poetry, dance and music. Its action typically brought royal or noble persons into association with the supernatural, thus affirming their connection to divinity.[3] Thus in Milton's masque 'the chief persons which presented, were The Lord Brackley, Mr Thomas Egerton his brother, The Lady Alice Egerton' as the Elder Brother, the Second Brother and the Lady respectively. The Lady's capture by the dionysian magician Comus, son of Bacchus and Circe, her defence of her virtue and her eventual rescue led by the Attendant Spirit in the guise of the Earl's shepherd follows this pattern precisely. We should note that neither the actor of the major role of the Spirit, who was played by the composer Henry Lawes, nor of Comus himself, who remains anonymous, were listed among the 'chief persons'. For all the complaisance of its genre, we can see how the masque contains the potential for chafing, if not conflict.

First, what *Princeton* describes as the masque's function 'to explore in a quasi-mystical way the sources and conditions of power' would, especially in seventeenth-century England, invite query rather than assent, perhaps not least among the artistic servitors themselves. 'There is no substitute for a rich man', wrote Hill in his ironic poem 'To the (Supposed) Patron' (*For the Unfallen*, 1959; *CP* p. 57), and he has always been keenly sensitive to what the age demands whether it is the flattery of wealth and power in Dryden's day (see 'Dryden's Prize-Song', *EC*) or of the '"Arts/Life" column' (*TL* XLVIII) of today's media markets. Among Hill's 'scenes' is a sidelong look at the cultural ramifications of masque that is not confined to its own time.

> Masques are booked to be simple, sensuous,
> comely, shaped to a fair design;
> not over-passionate;
> free from dark places and equivocation,
> present a tidy challenge, less to the maker
> than to the persons in the entertainment,
> young noble clones safely beset by clowns.
>
> (2.6)

Here Hill plays with Milton's own endorsement in *Of Education* of poetry as 'more simple, sensuous and passionate' than philosophy – an endorsement he has himself frequently quoted (see above, 'Acceptable words'). The nicety of its disruption by 'comely ... / not over-passionate' underscores the genteel character of masque, especially here where it must have been commissioned, at least in part, to indulge the children. The last line picks up on The Lady's opening speech in which she assumes that the noise of Comus's rout she hears is the 'ill-managed merriment' of 'the loose unlettered hinds', that is the local peasantry, or 'clowns'.

The inherited snobbery that associates them with what the audience knows to be a bestial, half-human company is acutely skewered in Hill's last line. So there are 'dark places and equivocation' in 'simple' masques, and the succeeding section probes them further.

> This our egregious masking – what it entails.
> Our sex-masques plague-threatened. Our murrain'd
> rustic to-and-fro-ing, lording it here, and there,
> craven in vanity. I mean, lawful
> lordship, powers that múst be, I do not grudge.
> Nor do I challenge the power of the Lord
> President in Cymru. *Diolch – diolch yn fawr!*
>
> (2.7)

This forelock-tugging to the egregious Egertons is palpably insincere. The 'sex-masques' possibly alludes to another likely motive for the Earl's commission which was that the Lady's display of exemplary, resolute virtue was intended to restore their reputation after the disgrace by association with a rape, prostitution and buggery scandal involving another branch of the family.[4] This is delicate matter and Milton had to be careful: 'I've not pieced out the story – Milton's script / was briefly censored, bits of sex expunged / for the girl's sake' (2.14). There is a sinister shadow round this child's-play as the fifteen-year-old Alice faces the seducer and her younger brothers homologise on chastity. Hill's register in this last quotation catches a bluff and crass modern tone – 'bits of sex', 'the girl' – that has a tabloid, or even a Larkinish, leer to it. He is revealing this 'egregious masking', but in this tone recognises something of our own debility. 'Our sex-masques plague-threatened' could almost be a shock-horror headline, denunciatory but itself part of the nature of present-day sexualisation that is 'murrain'd' (diseased) both literally and in its vanity and postures of control. So the fissure running through the Ludlow Masque in Geoffrey Hill's critique involves both social control and sexuality. The two can be seen to combine in the story that Hill glancingly refers to – not certainly substantiated – that Milton set his cap at the Lady Alice only to be put clearly in his place:

> the young commoner, Lawes's find, not found
> at the scene of his making, who might now
> be thought well worthy an earl's daughter.
>
> (2.16)

Whether or not this is true, respective power and weakness came numbingly home when 'the Younger Brother / said Milton should be topped,

his books burnt – / this over royalty and the republic' (2.72). In the next
century his descendant, Francis Egerton, Duke of Bridgewater, a major
investor in the burgeoning industrial revolution, was on the committee
that built the Grand Trunk Canal across these same lands.

> Look at our tangled I history. Neptune's
> forest submerging I compounding its coal measures,
> smoke-enriched England I her children ashen.
>
> (2.12)

Through the brilliant image of the compression of coal strata Hill connects
the mythological dimension of Milton's masque to the oxymoron of
wealth, pollution and deficiency of modern industrial England. Of course
Hill is not himself writing words for a masque. His 'Scenes ' are working
from the form, partly in homage to Milton's work and life, but also to dis-
rupt its stylised conventions by his own practice and uncover the social
relations behind the celebration: 'the sources and conditions of power':

> Milton meant civil war
> and civil detractions, and the sway of power,
>
> the pull of power, its *pondus*, its gravity.
>
> (1.14)

The second major dimension of the form of the masque I want to
consider in relation to *Scenes from Comus* is more closely aesthetic. As a
form combining words, music, dance and spectacle, masque must have
offered itself as a synthesised aesthetic experience to transcend what is
possible in any one of these genres alone. It is not difficult to see how-
ever that the achievement of such perfect balance might be anticipated
by tensions between them. If the form is 'substantially an invitation to a
dance' (*Princeton*), courtly attention to such close and intense argument
as Milton provides might not always have been assumed. For Ben Jonson
the theme and words of a masque were the work's 'soul', spectacle and
dance its body. His own conflicts with Inigo Jones testify to the inher-
ent tensions between the different aesthetics. As I have remarked above,
Hill often alludes to music in his work and figures poems after musical
forms. Elsewhere he emphasises his love and admiration for music of
many kinds from Dowland's lute to the bluegrass banjo.[5] As a dedication
to Hugh Wood's earlier work that adopts his title, *Scenes from Comus* can
surely be seen as a homage to the composer and to music itself. Yet the
truest homage to music can only be music. How does the work bear
upon the relation and difference between poetry and music?

At 1080 lines the whole is a comparable length to Milton's 'Comus', but the three parts of *Scenes from Comus* are divided by Hill's own configuration of the masque form:

1 The Argument of the Masque
2 Courtly Masquing Dances *nello stile antico*
3 A Description of the Antimasque.

The central 'Dances' are longer than 'The Argument' and the 'Antimasque' together in the ratio of exactly 3:2. Other symmetries are at least hinted at in that 1 and 3 are each comprised of twenty poems and part 2 of eighty. Each poem in 1 has ten lines grouped 3/3/3/1, each in 3 has twelve lines grouped 3/3/3/3. In the 'Dances' however the pattern uses odd numbers for undivided lengths in the sequence 9 7 7 9 9 7 7 and so on. On the epigraph page of the book, Hill quotes the twelve notes of the horn solo that opens Wood's *Scenes from Comus*. His own 1080 lines are exactly divisible by twelve in the proportion of nine, a number itself prominent in the poem as the ninth month of Michaelmas, in the 3 by 3 stanzas in 1, and the nine-line poems in 2.

These preliminary observations may prove more or less significant as study of the poem proceeds. If there is no mathematical or numerological structure underlying the series, then these patterns do at least point to an external shapeliness, an artifice presented as a pleasure to the reader which is analogous to the systems and intervals upon which music is based. In all successful art it is what Justus George Lawler in *Celestial Pantomime* calls 'the more or less unconsciously apprehended primordial structure'[6] that provides our pleasure over, and perhaps sometimes, against content. In poetry systematic form and sound will be the structural features most akin to music. Very early in the work Hill salutes Wood:

> Marvel at our contrary orbits. Mine
> salutes yours, whenever we pass or cross,
>
> which may be now, might very well be now.
>   (1.2)

But they are 'contrary orbits'. However poetry might aspire to the mathematical purity of non-mimetic structure, or sound unsullied by sense, it can never do so simply because with words reference is ineradicable. (Speaking of the relationship of poetry and music Hill has said that if a poem contains 'too much music' then it is not poetry.)[7] The first section of his masque immediately marks this out by announcing itself as 'The Argument' and pursuing an exaggeratedly discursive structure in which subjects are announced in the philosophical manner, 'Of the personality as a mask ... / Of licence and exorbitance ... / of custom and want of custom', and then with a series of assertions: 'That we are inordinate creatures ... / That this is no reason for us to despair ...' That he is parodying the procedural structures of philosophers such as Hobbes and Hume does not amount to a denial that 'argument' is entirely impossible in a poem. Rather it renders the effort of clarity that much more painful, even poignant:

> Language of occasion has here fallen
> into occurrence of outcry, reactive
> outcry, like a treatable depression
>
> that happens not to respond. If fate,
> then fated like autism. There is some notion,
> here, of the sea guffawing off reefs,
>
> to which we compose our daft music
> of comprehension. Rain-front on rain-front,
> then a sun-gash, clouds moody; the sea's mood
>
> turns from slate-black, to yellow ochre, to green.
>
> (1.4)

The deliberation of structured utterance, that which is called forth as appropriate to an occasion, breaks up under strain: occasion becomes ungovernable occurrence. In 1.2 we have already been told 'that we are / at once, rational, irrational – and there is reason', but here contingency strikes, defying the intervention of systematic reason: 'a treatable depression / that *happens not*' (my emphasis). The illustration of fate by autism points to mystery, that which confounds reason and especially strikes into language by the implication of its failure to achieve its commonly triumphant function to communicate and achieve empathy. Then, introduced with self-conscious diffidence – 'There is some notion, / here,' – the sea comes as a figure of the indifferent, even mocking real. The parenthetical commas around 'here', and the line-break, imply '*pause*, well, here anyway'. But the key word is 'guffawing'. The word puts us in mind of words commonly associated with breaking waves, 'roar', 'gulf', and might in itself be said to be onomatopoeic in the strong middle stress, 'guffawing'. The etymology is from the Scots 'gawf' or 'gaff' which is said by the OED to be onomatopoeic and also refers to loud boisterous laughter, glossing a phrase from Sinclair's *Satan's Invisible World* of 1678: 'the devil gave a great gaff of laughter'. Satan's laughter is indeed unlikely to be polite and it is the element of coarseness amounting almost to brutality, the sense that this kind of laugh is certainly at the expense of someone, that makes this metaphor so insidious. It is reminiscent of Wallace Stevens's 'the meaningless plungings of water and the wind' and 'Oh! Blessed rage for order, pale Ramon, / The maker's rage to order words of the sea' ('An Idea of Order at Key West'), but more inimical. But this is the background to which 'we compose our daft music / of comprehension'. There is both 'to' in the sense 'to the background of' but also in the sense of addressed to. This sense makes it poignantly quixotic, especially when set against the Attendant Spirit's invocation of the water-goddess Sabrina from 'Under the glassy, cool, translucent wave' to free the Lady from Comus's enchantment. In Milton's fantasy the Spirit calls upon 'the power of some adjuring verse' that Sabrina might 'Listen and save'. And so she does, for 'Comus' is a profound myth of recuperation, and specifically of the instruments of healing. Sabrina sings:

> Brightest Lady look on me,
> Thus I sprinkle on thy breast
> Drops that from my fountain pure,
> I have kept of precious cure[.]
> (*Comus* ll. 909–12)

Previously the Spirit and the Brothers were able to put Comus to flight with the aid of haemony, 'a small unsightly root, / But of divine effect'. Hill makes much of haemony in a sequence in the 'Dances', 2.9-12. First its curative properties are like a miracle drug of spiritual power which

> melts like a pearl,
> chemical self-renewal not to be paid for,
> retroactively inheres, working forgiveness
> within the act,
>
> (2.9)

then,

> Suppose I tell it otherwise: haemony
> is of the blood (therefore the lovely name);
> the elect possess it, subject to possession;
> it cannot be bought, bartered, part exchanged.
> (2.10)

Finally comes this prickly 'dim prodigy / uncultivated / and of glummest fruition' (Hill is following Milton's description, 'darkish, and had prickles on it ... / Unknown and like esteemed' exactly here, see l. 628–36).

> Haemony may mean technē | now he tells me.
> Haemony means whatever Milton | meánt by it.
> (2.12)

This is the same section that takes us to Bridgewater's technology and 'smoke-enriched England'. For Hill haemony 'means' transformation, hopefully curative, but is so mysterious that as technē it is always going to be uncertain. But always there is a dream of recuperation. 'Simples', including haemony, but also others – woundwort, centaury, horehound –recur in *The Orchards of Syon* (see VIII, IX, XIV, XIX, LVI), and *The Triumph of Love* CXV closes:

> (End with that reference, in the Ludlow masque,
> to *haemony*, plant of exilic virtue.)

They are 'unknown, and like esteemed', yet comforting, at least in their possibility. Like their successor, 'the signal / mystery, mercy' of serotonin (*TL* CIX), they might also work spiritually so as to heal guilt, 'working forgiveness / into the act'. Yet none of this has the swift expedition of the Attendant Spirit's haemony, or of Sabrina's song. Outside of the desirable myth things are 'like a treatable depression / that happens not to respond'. Yet what are we to make of this beautiful word 'daft': 'to which we compose our daft music / of comprehension'? The top line of understanding will be that poet and composer seek 'comprehension' of the flux of occurrence, that the ordering of art will bring it within our compass. But those ungovernable waves in their 'guffawing' incoherence make clear that this is a stupid idea. However, 'daft' does not simply mean stupid. Its earliest Old English meanings are 'mild, gentle, meek, humble', only later acquiring the connotations of 'wanting in intelligence, stupid, foolish', and later still 'of unsound mind, crazy, insane, mad'. As the *OED* makes clear, within the Old English root was contained the sense of 'becoming, fit, suitable': 'the primary meaning of the adjective must have been "becoming, fit"'. In Middle English these senses seem to have migrated to the closely cousined word 'deft'. This history of the word does encourage the view that these senses of 'gentle', 'fitting' and 'deft' are effective in this 'daft music'. But I don't think the interpretation relies wholly on excavation through the *OED*. Even in common present-day usage, 'daft' ('now chiefly *Sc.* and *north*' (*OED*) and thus 'little esteemed') carries the senses of geniality, innocence, giddiness. To say 'don't be so daft' is not a scornful rebuke, and to acknowledge that one is 'daft to do it' implies acting against one's own best interests. Hill and Wood might be said to be 'daft to do it', but they do. Thus this one word counters the direction of the sentence. Yet the perplexity brought by the world's unpredictable contingencies is then brilliantly evoked in the next three lines:

> Rain-front on rain-front,
> then a sun-gash, clouds moody; the sea's mood
>
> turns from slate-black, to yellow ochre, to green.
>
> (1.4)

The flicker from the phraseology of meteorology here guys the crucial scientific notion of predictability just as the other words show us this changeability. It is in such realisations that we see that the effort of 'comprehension' in such 'wordly' ways is not so daft after all.

The final proposition in 'The Argument' is

> That weight of the world, weight of the word, is.
>
> (1.20)

When Jonson wrote of the words of the masque as its soul he must have meant that they transcend earth-bound dance and spectacle. For Hill words do not fly up but are strongly held by gravity. Through Milton I want now to explore the matter of the ascent and obduracy of words along the axis of flesh and spirit.

In 'Comus' the Elder Brother seeks to reassure his younger brother that their sister's resolute purity will be able to withstand any assault because heaven will come to her aid and

> Tell her of things that no gross ear can hear,
> Till oft converse with heavenly habitants
> Begin to cast a beam on the outward shape,
> The unpolluted temple of the mind,
> And turns it by degrees to the soul's essence,
> Till all be made immortal[.]
>
> (ll. 457–62)

Milton's editor John Carey notes that this chimes with 'the doctrine of the transformation of flesh into spirit' (*CSP* p. 199) as Milton later propounded it in Raphael's speech to Adam in Book V of *Paradise Lost*. Here he instructs Adam in the different kinds of being in earth and heaven, of himself and of angels. It is a strongly Platonic ascent 'till body up to spirit work' and he uses this analogy:

> So from the root
> Springs lighter the green stalk, from thence the leaves
> More airy, last the bright consummate flower
> Spirits odorous breathes: flowers and their fruit
> Man's nourishment, by gradual scale sublimed
> To vital spirits aspire, to animal,
> To intellectual, give both life and sense,

Fancy and understanding, whence the soul
Reason receives, and reason is her being,
Discursive, or intuitive; discourse
Is oftest yours, the latter most is ours,
Differing but in degree, of kind the same.

(ll. 479–90)

Though 'time may come when men / With angels may participate', human words are 'discursive' not 'intuitive', fleshly not spiritual, unless, for Milton, they are powered by the transformative purity exemplified by The Lady, or such moments as the 'heavenly infant's birth' when 'My muse with angels did divide to sing' ('The Passion' ll. 3–4). But if words are held down, what of music? In 'Comus' the Attendant Spirit speaks of hearing the Lady's Song:

At last a soft and solemn-breathing sound
Rose like a steam of rich distilled perfumes,
And stole upon the air, that even Silence
Was took ere she was ware, and wished she might
Deny her nature, and be never more
Still to be so displaced. I was all ear,
And took in strains that might create a soul
Under the ribs of death[.]

(ll. 554–61)

Here music is likened to the unbodied perfumes Raphael speaks of and is imbued with the power 'that might create a soul / Under the ribs of death'. Mere words remain below.

The association of language and the material world and therefore corruption is an ancient and powerful idea and one that preoccupies Hill. In *The Triumph of Love* he ponders the conjoining of 'grammar and the Fall' (CXXXIX). In 'The Argument' of *Scenes from Comus* he uses three times the Latin word *pondus*, which in English usage means not only weight but 'power to influence … moral force'. It is the weight of 'moral corruption', 'inertia of malevolence, or *pondus*' (1.6). Second, in 1.14 the poet looks over the north Atlantic:

Gloam lies pulsing
at the sea-skyline, where the *Hood* blew up
surging at full speed, a kind of wake

over the sudden mass grave foul with cordite,
gradually settling. Milton meant civil war
and civil detractions, and the sway of power,

the pull of power, its *pondus*, its gravity.

Hill carefully associates 'the pull of power' with the *pondus* of the battleship 'gradually settling'. The third moment is both comic and more personal in the proposition 'That actors think too highly of themselves. / O damn this *pondus* of splenetic pride!' (1.17). All of these bear the insistence upon weight, pulls of differing kinds but all part of 'that weight of the world' and so 'weight of the word': 'Almost we cannot pull free; almost we escape // the leadenness of things' (1.20).

'Music arguably / not implicated in the loss of Eden, / held to its resolution', muses Hill in *The Orchards of Syon* VII. Can it make sense to say that music is 'innocent'? As against poetry perhaps it can more readily 'pull free … escape / … the leadenness of things'. Throughout *Scenes from Comus* there is an alternation between weight and lightness, the narrow intervals of light and darkness at the 'wintry solstice'. The poem seeks an assertion within its own nature:

> There is a dogged beauty in the world,
> unembarrassing goodness, honesty unfazed.
> There's also the corrupter, the abuser,
> the abused corrupted in accepted ways,
> the ways of death, the deadliness of life.
>
> (2.25)

'Dogged beauty' and corruption inhere in the poet's medium and in the struggle between them he is on his own.

11 Afterword: "'I have not finished'"

> Something here even so. Our well dug-in
> language pitches us as it finds –
> I tell myself
> don't wreck a good phrase simply to boost sense –
> granted its dark places, the fabled burden;
> its loops and extraordinary progressions,
> its mere conundrums forms and rites of discourse;
> its bleak littoral swept by bursts of sunlight;
> its earthen genius auditing the spheres.

In this closing passage of 'Discourse: For Stanley Rosen'[1] I want to dwell on the penultimate line: 'its bleak littoral swept by bursts of sunlight'. The littoral has held a powerful place in Geoffrey Hill's poetic imagination right from the beginning. The seashore and tracts between water and land appear recurrently in *For the Unfallen*. In 'Genesis' the speaker sees 'The osprey plunge with triggered claw, / Feathering blood along the shore'. It is bleak too in 'Requiem for the Plantaganet Kings' where 'the sea / Across daubed rock evacuates its dead.' In 'The Guardians' the old 'wade the disturbed shore; / Gather the dead as the first dead scrape home.' In 'Doctor Faustus' there is a 'torn *Warning to bathers* / By the torn waters.' 'Metamorphoses 5' evokes a 'sun-clouded marshworld and strewn sea', and sunlight breaks through elsewhere as in 'After Cumae': 'The sun again unearthed, colours come up fresh'. It is a blessing in 'Orpheus and Eurydice' where there is 'the rare pale sun / To water our days'. In 'Little Apocalypse' though, the sun is less mild in its 'primitive renewing fury', and in 'A Prayer to the Sun' from *King Log* it is 'our ravager', though its blessing is sought 'so that we sleep'. Later, in *The Triumph of Love* the touches of light, however evanescent and tentative, reveal intimations of 'real Being': 'the hedged sun / draws into itself for its self-quenching' (XXXVIII). Elsewhere in the poem memory is cared for 'in this tranche of frozen sunlight' (XCII). In *Speech! Speech!* there is 'Again: the saltmarsh in winter' (81), and later 'A pale full sun, draining its winter light, / illuminates the bracken and the bracken coloured / leaves of stubborn oak' (102).

We cannot fathom why particular images unfold within, or snag, a poet's imagination. The 'bleak littoral' is by no means Hill's only landscape but it appeals, and our response as readers will first be gratitude for these realisations in words – '*swept* by burst of sunlight'. Shore and marsh and light can be readily constructed as thematic metaphors: a pitiless sun reveals desolation, a milder sun touches it with consolation. But in 'Discourse: For Stanley Rosen' littoral and sunlight work as a metaphor for 'well dug-in language' itself. All of Hill's work in the tilth of language knows that metaphor is but one instance of its approximate nature, that it 'pitches us as it finds'. But his wintry, hedged, clouded , 'rare pale' sunlights might sometimes pitch him, and so his readers, beyond labouring.

> ÁND ׀ ís this vision enough ׀ unnamed, unknown
> bird of immediate flight, of estuaries?

Notes

1 'Acceptable words'

1 John Milton, 'Of Education', *Selected Prose*, ed. C. A. Patrides, (Harmondsworth, 1974), p. 191.

2 Thomas Sprat, *The History of the Royal Society of London for the Improving of Natural Knowledge*, (1667) p. 43; George Berkeley, *Treatise concerning the Principles of Human Knowledge*, (1710); Isaac Barrow, attributed. All these quotations are drawn from Roy Porter, *Enlightenment, Britain and the Creation of the Modern World*, (London, 2000), pp. 54–5.

3 Thomas Hobbes: see *Leviathan*, part I, chapter 4, 'Of Speech'.

4 T. S. Eliot, *Four Quartets*, (London, 1959), 'Burnt Norton', ll. 149–53.

5 Geoffrey Hill, 'The Art of Poetry LXXX', *Paris Review*, 154, Spring 2000, p. 277.

6 Ezra Pound, 'Hugh Selwyn Mauberley (Life and Contacts)', *Selected Poems*, (London, 1975), p. 101.

7 Walter Benjamin, 'Theses on the Philosophy of History VII', translated by Harry Zohn, *Illuminations*, (London, 1973) p. 258.

8 Geoffrey Hill, 'I. Intrinsic Value: Marginal Observations on a Central Question', *Rhetorics of Value*, The Tanner Lectures on Human Values, delivered at Brasenose College, Oxford, 6 and 7 March 2000, p. 259. Full text available at www.tannerlectures. utah.edu/lectures/Hill_01.pdf.

9 John Dunn, 'Political Obligation', *The History of Political Theory and Other Essays*, (Cambridge, 1996), p. 87.

10 For a fine discussion of Hill's use of popular comedy see John Lyon, '"What are you incinerating?": Geoffrey Hill and Popular Culture', *English*, 2005.

11 Daniel Green, *Great Cobbett, the Noblest Agitator*, (Oxford, 1985), p. 460.

12 Porter, *Enlightenment*, p. 482.

13 See Hill on the 'difficulty' of poetry and the difficulty of life. 'One encounters in any ordinary day far more real difficulty than one confronts in the most "intellectual" piece of work', *Paris Review*, pp. 276–7. See also for a consideration of 'how difficult a word like "difficult" really is', Peter McDonald, 'Difficulty, Democracy, and Modern Poetry', *PN Review161*, Vol. 31 No. 3, January–February 2005, pp. 19–24.

14 Geoffrey Hill, 'Carnal Policy *i.m. Ken Smith*', *Stand*, Vol. 6 No. 1, Spring 2005, pp. 10–11.

2 'The speechless dead': *King Log* (1968)

1 Bruce Catton, *The Penguin Book of the American Civil War*, (Harmondsworth, 1966), p. 64.

2 Ricks draws upon this article from *The London Magazine*, November 1964, in Christopher Ricks, 'Clichés', *The Force of Poetry*, (New York, 1984), pp. 356–68.
3 William Wordsworth, '*Preface* to Lyrical Ballads', 1802, in John O. Hayden, ed., *The Poems Volume One*, (Harmondsworth, 1977), p. 879.
4 Ezra Pound, 'Vers Libre and Arnold Dolmetsch', *Literary Essays of Ezra Pound*, edited and introduced by T. S. Eliot, (London, 1960), p. 440.
5 Geoffrey Hill: 'Averroism was the doctrine of monopsychism, that is that there's only one single Intellect, or "intellective" soul for the whole of humanity, and it seemed to me at first sight a most comforting doctrine – the idea that all kinds of personal guilt, a burden of culpability for all eternity, might be absorbed and absolved in that one "Intellect" – but afterwards I felt it was not a doctrine to be embraced at all; it seemed to be the archetype of the totalitarian state ... The attraction of what I came to see as its specious comfort and also of its coldness is captured in that metaphor, which – if I can say so – managed to be quite beautiful while at the same time being an image of a beautiful coldness and desolation.'
From John Haffenden, *Viewpoints: Poets in Conversation*, (London, 1981), p. 98.

3 Poet, lover, liar: 'Lachrimae' (1975)

1 A. O. Meyer, *England and the Catholic Church under Elizabeth*, (1914) (London, 1967), p. 217.
2 Thomas Mann, *Doctor Faustus*, 1947; tr. H. T. Lowe-Porter, (Harmondsworth, 1968), p. 63.
3 '"The Conscious Mind's Intelligible Structure": A Debate', *Agenda*, Vol. 9 No. 4 – Vol. 10 No. 1, Autumn–Winter 1971–72, pp. 14–23 (not collected).
4 Herbert Marcuse, *An Essay on Liberation*, 1969, (Harmondsworth: Pelican, 1972) p. 50. My attention was first drawn to this passage by a friend and colleague, Alf Louvre, though he is in no way to be held responsible for any comments upon it I make here.
5 Diana Poulton, *John Dowland*, (Berkeley, 1972), p. 124.
6 Mann, *Doctor Faustus*, p. 311.
7 Hill, '"The Conscious Mind's Intelligible Structure"'.
8 J. M. Cohen, ed. *The Penguin Book of Spanish Verse*, (Harmondsworth, 1960), p. 247, for Spanish text and prose translation of this sonnet.

4 'Our love is what we love to have': *Tenebrae* (1978)

1 Henri Focillon, *Art of the West 1: Romanesque*, (Oxford, 1963), p. 6.
2 *Paul Celan: Poems*, selected, translated and with an introduction by Michael Hamburger, (Manchester, 1980), p. 143.
3 Sidney Keyes, 'Sour Land III', *Collected Poems*, ed. Michael Meyer, (Manchester, 2002), p. 14.
4 Harold Bloom, 'Introduction – The Survival of Strong Poetry' to the American collection of Hill's poetry, *Somewhere Is Such a Kingdom, Poems 1952–1971*, (Boston, 1975), p. xiv.
5 See Geoffrey Hill's article 'Redeeming the Time': 'If language is more than a vehicle for the transmission of axioms and concepts, rhythm is correspondingly

more than a physiological motor. It is capable of registering, mimetically, deep shocks of recognition.' *LL*, p. 87.

6   Owen Barfield, *History in English Words*, (London, 1962), p. 103.

7   R. O. Jones, *A Literary History of Spain: The Golden Age*, London, 1971, pp. 87–8.

8   *Agenda*, Vol. 10 No. 4 – Vol. 11 No. 1, Autumn–Winter 1972–73, p. 68.

9   Barfield, *History*, ch. VII.

10 Hill describes the development of 'The Pentecost Castle', first out of music by the sixteenth-century composer Antonio de Cabezón, and then through poems by Lope de Vega in his interview in Haffenden, *Viewpoints*, pp. 91–3.

11 'muddled dreaming' is a phrase adapted from Hill: 'Where, sensitive and half-under a cloud, / Europe muddles her dreaming ...'; 'The Martyrdom of Saint Sebastian', *For the Unfallen*, *CP* p. 51.

5 Things and words:
The Mystery of the Charity of Charles Péguy (1983)

The Mystery of the Charity of Charles Péguy, 1983, is included in *Collected Poems* at pp. 183–96, and *New and Collected Poems 1952–1992*, at pp. 163–9. Substantial quotations in this essay refer to the sections of the poem.

1   The words of the epigraph are Péguy's, quoted by Julien Green in his introduction to the selection of Péguy's work *Basic Verities: Prose and Poetry*, 'rendered into English by Ann and Julien Green', (London, 1943), p. 36.

2   J. L. Austin, *How to Do Things With Words*, ed. J. O. Urmson, Second Edition, (Oxford, 1965), hereafter *Words*.

3   See Hill's note to the poem 'Charles Péguy': 'a young madman, who may or may not have been over-susceptible to metaphor, almost immediately shot Jaurès through the head'. *CP* p. 206.

4   Quoted in Marjorie Villiers, *Charles Péguy: A Study in Integrity*, (London, 1965), p. 290.

5   Henri Bergson, *Creative Evolution*, trans. Arthur Mitchell, 1911, (New York: 1944; Westport, Ct, 1975), pp. 7, 23.

6   See John Terraine, *The Great War 1914–18*, (London, 1965): 'At all levels French soldiers were taught the virtues of headlong attack' (p. 20). Terraine remarks on the 'lavish spending' of French officers' lives in the early days of the war (p. 48). Also, John Ellis, *Eye Deep in Hell: Trench Warfare in World War I*, (London and New York, 1976) writes of 'a kind of military "spiritualism", a continual stress upon human capabilities at the expense of the potential of material forces'. He quotes Joffre in 1912: 'The French Army, returning to its traditions, no longer knows any other law than that of the offensive' (pp. 82–4).

7   Charles Péguy, *Oeuvres Poétiques Complètes*, (Paris, 1967); the passage is also in *The Penguin Book of French Verse 4: The Twentieth Century*, edited and introduced by Anthony Hartley, (Harmondsworth, 1966), p. 90.

8   *Harrap's Shorter French and English Dictionary*, ed. J. E. Mansion (London, 1960).

9   See *LL* p. 159 where Hill quotes Pound: 'And when one has the mot juste, one is finished with the subject.'

10 Roland Barthes, *Elements of Semiology*, (1964) trans. Annette Lavers and Colin
    Smith, (Boston, 1967), pp. 88, 86.

11 Jonathan Culler, *Structuralist Poetics*, (London, 1975), p. 130.

12 Hill is quoting from Ransom, *The New Criticism*, (Norfolk, Ct, 1941), p. 79.

13 Paul Ricoeur, *The Rule of Metaphor*, trans. Robert Czerny et al., (London, 1978),
    p. 115.

14 Daniel Halévy, *Péguy et Les Cahiers de la Quinzaine*, (Paris, 1941), p. 188; my
    translation.

15 Henri Bergson, *Time and Free Will*, trans. F. L. Pogson, (London, 1910; New
    York, 1912), p. 209.

16 Hill is quoting Kenneth Burke, *A Grammar of Motives*, (New York, 1945),
    p. 491.

6 History as poetry:
'Churchill's Funeral' and 'De Jure Belli ac Paris' (*Canaan, 1996*)

1 Edward Elgar, *Letters to 'Nimrod'*, ed. Percy M. Young, (London, 1965), p. 113.

2 Alec Harman and Wilfrid Mellers, *Man and His Music*, (London, 1962),
   p. 967.

3 John Ruskin, *Unto this Last & Other Essays on Art & Political Economy*, (London,
   1907), p. 110.

4 Richard Hough, *Winston & Clementine, The Triumph of the Churchills*, (London,
   1990), pp. 536, 538.

5 Quoted in Michael Baigent and Richard Leigh, *Secret Germany: Claus von
   Stauffenberg and the Mystical Crusade Against Hitler*, (London, 1994), p. 64.

6 *Agenda*, Vol. 32 No. 2, Summer 1994, p. 12.

7 Quoted in Ger van Roon, *German Resistance to Hitler: Count von Moltke and the
   Kreisau Circle*, 1967, (London, 1971), p. 54.

8 Hermann Graml, 'Resistance Thinking on Foreign Policy', in Graml et al., *The
   German Resistance to Hitler*, 1966, (London, 1970), p. 31.

9 Gillian Rose, *Love's Work*, (London, 1995), p. 116.

10 Martha Nussbaum, *The Fragility of Goodness: Luck and Ethics in Greek Tragedy
    and Philosophy*, (Cambridge, 1986), p. 314.

7 The Triumph of Love (1998)

1 'Although salvation …': Petrarch, *Familiarum rerum libri*, 17,1,3, quoted by
   Stephen Minta, *Petrarch and Petrarchism: The English and French Traditions*,
   (Manchester, 1980), p. 101.

2 *Lord Morley's* Tryumphes of Fraunces Petrarcke, *The First English Translation of
   the* Trionfi, ed. D. D. Carnicelli, (Cambridge, Mass., 1971).

3 *TLS*, 29 January 1999, p. 8.

4 Brian Vickers, *In Defence of Rhetoric*, (Oxford, 1988), p. 65.

5 *The New Princeton Encyclopedia of Poetry and Poetics*, 1993, 'Rhetoric and
   Poetry', p. 1047.

6 Vickers, *In Defence of Rhetoric*, p. 62.

7 Vickers, *In Defence of Rhetoric*, p. 21.

8 *Thus Spoke Zarathrustra*, translated by R. J. Hollingdale, (Harmondsworth, 1969), p. 46; the passage comes to my attention via Martha Nussbaum's *The Fragility of Goodness*, p. 163.

9 My sources for this summary include *Encyclopaedia Britannica* and Simon Blackburn, *The Oxford Dictionary of Philosophy*, (Oxford and New York, 1994).

10 Ludwig Wittgenstein, *Tractatus Logico-Philosophicus*, 1921; trans. D. F. Pears and B. F. McGuinness, (London, 1961).

11 Blackburn, *The Oxford Dictionary of Philosophy*, p. 246.

8 'Beauty is difficult': *Speech! Speech!* (2000)

1 Ezra Pound, Canto LXXIV, *The Cantos of Ezra Pound*, (London, 1964), p. 472.

2 Letter to James Joyce, *Pound/Joyce: The Letters of Ezra Pound to James Joyce, with Pound's Essays on Joyce*, ed. F. Reed (London, 1968), p. 122; quoted by Hill in *The Enemy's Country*, p. 94.

3 'PROJECTIVE VERSE', in Donald M. Allen, ed., *The New American Poetry 1945–60*, (New York, 1960), p. 388.

4 *Gaudier-Brzeska: A Memoir*, (1916) (London, 1960).

5 Alan Wall, 'Geoffrey Hill's *Canaan*', *Agenda*, Vol. 34 No. 2, Summer 1996, p. 36.

6 Charles Taylor, *Sources of the Self: The Making of Modern Identity*, (Cambridge, 1989) p. 466.

7 Honoré Daumier, *Honoré Daumier 40 Lithographs*, selected and edited by Wilhelm Wartmann, translated by Harry N. Schnur (Zurich, Manesse Verlag Conzett & Huber), p. 211.

8 Dietrich Bonhoeffer, *Letters and Papers from Prison*, an abridged edition, ed. Eberhard Bethge (London, 1981), pp. 88–9.

9 Geoffrey Hill, 'I. Intrinsic Value: Marginal Observations on a Central Question', *RV* pp. 265–6.

10 I am grateful to my friend Dr. John Davidson, a historian of West Africa, for a summary of events and information about the individuals who feature in these poems.

11 Hartley, ed., *The Penguin Book of French Verse 4: The Twentieth Century*, p. 279.

12 *RV* p. 266.

13 *RV* p. 259. See above, 'Chapter 1, for a more extended consideration of Hill and Hobbes's *Leviathan*.

14 Tom Wolfe, *The Bonfire of the Vanities*, (New York, 1987).

9 Here and there I pull a flower: *The Orchards of Syon* (2002)

1 Robert Burton, *The Anatomy of Melancholy* (1621), edited and introduced by Holbrook Jackson, (Everyman, London, 1972).

2 Geoffrey Hill, 'The Art of Poetry LXXX', *Paris Review*, 154, Spring 2000, p. 292.

3 Frank O'Hara, *Selected Poems*, ed. Donald Allen, (Manchester: 1991), p. 174.

4 See Hill's discussion of Hopkins's vocabulary in 'Redeeming the Time', *LL*, especially pp. 97–103, and 'Common Weal, Common Woe', *SF*, especially pp. 2–4.

5 Christopher Ricks, 'Clichés', *The Force of Poetry*, pp. 356–68.

6 *Paris Review*, pp. 282–3.

7 *Paul Celan: Poems*, p. 203.

8 *EC*, p. 93 & 102; Hill is quoting from Ezra Pound, 'Notes on Elizabethan Classicists', *Literary Essays* (London, 1954), p. 241.

10 'In wintry solstice like the shorten'd light': *Scenes from Comus* (2005)

1 John Milton, *Complete Shorter Poems*, ed. John Carey, (London, 1968).

2 *Scenes from Comus* is composed in three parts with numbered sections within each part. References here are to part and section, e.g. 2.80 etc.

3 For a summary account see the entry 'Masque' in *The New Princeton Encyclopedia of Poetry and Poetics*, edited by Alex Preminger and T. V. P. Brogan, (Princeton, 1993). Hereafter *Princeton*.

4 See Christopher Hill, *Milton and the English Revolution*, (London, 1977), pp. 43–4.

5 Interview with David Yezzi, *The New York Sun*, 7 November 2002. Also see note 7 below.

6 Justus George Lawler, *Celestial Pantomime, Poetic Structures of Transcendence*, (New York, 1994), p. 88.

7 *Private Passions*, conversation with Michael Berkeley, BBC Radio 3, 25 April 2004.

Afterword: "'I have not finished'"

1 Published in *The New Criterion*, Vol. 21 No. 10, June 2003; *Without Title*, 2006.

Select bibliography

Works by Geoffrey Hill

Poetry

For the Unfallen, Poems 1952–1958, (London: André Deutsch, 1959).

King Log, (London: André Deutsch, 1968).

Mercian Hymns, (London: André Deutsch, 1971).

Somewhere Is Such a Kingdom, Poems 1952–1971, *(Boston: Houghton Mifflin, 1971)*.

Tenebrae, (London: André Deutsch, 1978).

The Mystery of the Charity of Charles Péguy, (London: Agenda Editions and André Deutsch, 1983).

Collected Poems, (Harmondsworth: Penguin Books, 1985).

New and Collected Poems 1952–1992, (Boston: Houghton Mifflin, 1994).

Canaan, (Harmondsworth: Penguin Books, 1996; Boston: Houghton Mifflin, 1997).

The Triumph of Love: A Poem, (Boston: Houghton Mifflin, 1998; Harmondsworth: Penguin Books, 1999).

Speech! Speech!, (Washington, D.C: Counterpoint; London: Penguin Books, 2000).

The Orchards of Syon, (Washington, D.C: Counterpoint; London: Penguin Books, 2002).

Scenes from Comus, (London: Penguin Books, 2005).

A Treatise of Civil Power, (Oxford: Clutag Press, 2005).

Without Title, (London: Penguin Books, 2006).

Poetic drama

Brand (Henrik Ibsen), A Version for the English Stage, (London: Heinemann & The National Theatre, 1978; Second edition, University of Minnesota Press, 1981; A Version for the Stage, Harmondsworth: Penguin Books, 1996).

Prose

'"I in Another Place." Homage to Keith Douglas', *Stand*, Vol. 6 No 4, no date, pp 6–13, (not collected).

'The Poetry of Allen Tate', *Geste*, Vol. 3 No. 3, November, 1958, pp. 8–12, (not collected).

'"The Conscious Mind's Intelligible Structure": A Debate', *Agenda*, Vol. 9 No. 4 – Vol. 10 No. 1, Autumn–Winter 1971–2, pp. 14–23 (not collected).

'Gurney's "Hobby"', F. W. Bateson Memorial Lecture, *Essays in Criticism*, Vol. XXXIV, No. 2 April 1984, pp. 97–128.

Review: *The Life of John Berryman* by John Haffenden; *Poets in their Youth: A Memoir* by Eileen Simpson, *Essays in Criticism*, Vol. XXXIV No. 3, July 1984, pp. 262–9.

The Lords of Limit: Essays on Literature and Ideas, (London: André Deutsch, 1984).

The Enemy's Country: Words, Contexture, and Other Circumstances of Language, (Oxford: Clarendon Press, 1991).

Rhetorics of Value, The Tanner Lectures on Human Values, delivered at Brasenose College, Oxford, 6 and 7 March 2000. Full text available at www.tannerlectures.utah.edu/lectures/Hill_01.pdf.

Style and Faith, (New York: Counterpoint, 2003).

Interviews

'Blake Morrison interviews Geoffrey Hill', *The New Statesman*, 8 February 1980, pp. 212–14.

Viewpoints: Poets in Conversation, John Haffenden interviews Geoffrey Hill (London: Faber & Faber, 1981).

'David Sexton talks to Geoffrey Hill', *The Literary Review*, No. 28, February 1986.

'Poet Geoffrey Hill wins the Kahn Award for *Canaan*.' Eric McHenry talks to Geoffrey Hill about the award. *BU Bridge*, Vol. 1, No. 32, 5 June 1998.

'The Art of Poetry LXXX', an interview with Geoffrey Hill, *Paris Review*, No. 154, Spring 2000.

Eric McHenry talks to Geoffrey Hill and Christopher Ricks about the T. S. Eliot Award', *BU Bridge*, Vol. IV No. 8, 6 October 2000.

'Meaningful Speech', *Publishers Weekly*. Steve Burt interviews Geoffrey Hill, Issue 14, 8 April 2002.

Robert Potts, 'The Praise Singer' – Profile, *The Guardian* (London), 10 August 2002.

'David Yezzi talks to Geoffrey Hill at his home in Mass., USA', *The New York Sun*, 7 November 2002.

Private Passions, conversation with Michael Berkeley, BBC Radio 3, 25 April 2004.

Websites

Geoffrey Hill Study Center: www3.sympatico.ca/sylvia.paul/geoffrey_hill_index.htm

Université de Caen (in French and English): www.unicaen.fr/mrsh/anglais/geoffrey-hill

Secondary texts

Agenda, special issues: Vol. 13 No. 3, Autumn 1975; Vol. 17 No. 1, Spring 1979; Vol. 30 Nos 1–2, Spring–Summer 1992; Vol. 34 No. 2, Summer 1996.

Bedient, Calvin, "The Pastures of Wilderness: Geoffrey Hill's 'An Apology for the Revival of Christian Architecture in England'", *Yearbook of English Studies,* Vol. 17 (1987), pp. 143–65.

Bedient, Calvin, 'On Geoffrey Hill', *Critical Quarterly,* Vol. 23 No. 2 (1981), pp. 17–26.

Bloom, Harold, 'Introduction – the Survival of Strong Poetry', Geoffrey Hill, *Somewhere Is Such a Kingdom, Poems 1952–1971,* (Boston: Houghton Mifflin, 1975); also in Bloom, *Figures of Capable Imagination,* (New York: Continuum, 1976).

Donoghue, Denis, '"Lover of Lost Cause", *Canaan* and *The Triumph of Love',* *NYRB,* 29 May 1999.

Edwards, Michael, 'Quotidian epic: Geoffrey Hill's *The Triumph of Love',* *Yale Journal of Criticism,* Vol. 13 No. 1 (2000): pp. 167–76.

Ehrenpreis, Irvin, Review of *Somewhere Is Such a Kingdom, NYRB,* 22 January 1976.

Gervais, David, 'A New Direction: Essay-review on Geoffrey Hill', *The Reader,* Issue 11, 2002.

Hart, Henry, *The Poetry of Geoffrey Hill,* (Carbondale: Southern Illinois University Press, 1986).

Heaney, Seamus, 'Englands of the Mind', *Preoccupations: Selected Prose, 1968–1978* (London: Faber & Faber, 1980).

Heaney, Seamus, *Finders Keepers: Selected Prose 1971–2001,* (London: Faber & Faber, 2002).

Horner, Avril, *Geoffrey Hill: English Modernist or Post Modern European?* (University of Salford, European Studies Research Institute, January 1994).

Horner, Avril, 'The "Intelligence at Bay": Ezra Pound and Geoffrey Hill', Orono: *Paideuma,* Vol. 22 Nos 1–2, (1993), pp. 243–54.

Kerrigan, John, 'Divided Kingdoms and the Local Epic: *Mercian Hymns* to *The King of Britain's Daughter',* *The Yale Journal of Criticism,* Vol. 13 No. 1 (2000).

Kilgore, Jennifer, '"Fierce tea-making/in time of war": English Heritage and the War in Geoffrey Hill's "Churchill's Funeral"', *les Actes du Colloque HERITAGES* (Collection Cahiers du GREAM, Le Mans, 2000), pp. 72–103.

Kilgore, Jennifer, 'Seeking "the root in justice": Geoffrey Hill on Ezra Pound', in Hélène Aji (ed.), *Ezra Pound and Referentiality,* (Paris: Presses de l'Université de Paris-Sorbonne, 2003), pp. 93–103.

Kirsch, Adam, Review of *The Triumph of Love, TLS,* 29 January 1999, pp. 7–8.

Knottenbelt, E. M., *Passionate Intelligence: The Poetry of Geoffrey Hill* (Amsterdam and Atlanta: Rodopi, 1990).

Lyon, John, '"Pardon?" Our Problem with Difficulty (and Geoffrey Hill)',
    Thumbscrew, No. 13 (1999), pp. 11–19.
Lyon, John, '"What are you incinerating?" Geoffrey Hill and Popular
    Culture', *English*, 2005.
Milne, W. S., *An Introduction to Geoffrey Hill* (London: Agenda/Bellew
    Publishing, 1998).
McDonald, Peter, 'The Pitch of Dissent: Geoffrey Hill', in *Serious Poetry:*
    Form and Authority from Yeats to Hill (Oxford: Oxford University
    Press, 2002).
McDonald, Peter, 'Pulling Through' (on *The Orchards of Syon*), *Literary*
    Imagination: The Review of the Association of Literary Scholars and
    Critics, Vol. 5 No. 2, 2003.
McDonald, Peter, 'Difficulty, Democracy, and Modern Poetry', *PN Review*
    161, Vol. 31 No. 3 (January–February 2005), pp. 19–24.
Paulin, Tom, 'A Visionary Nationalist: Geoffrey Hill', *Minotaur* (London:
    Faber & Faber, 1992).
Ricks, Christopher, 'Geoffrey Hill 1: "The tongue's atrocities"'; 'Geoffrey
    Hill 2: "At-one-ment"', pp. 285–355; 'Clichés', pp. 261–5, *The Force*
    of Poetry, (Oxford: Oxford University Press, 1984).
Roberts, Andrew Michael, *Geoffrey Hill: Writers and Their Work* (Tavistock:
    British Council & Northcote House Educational Publishers, 2004).
Robinson, Peter (ed.), *Geoffrey Hill: Essays on His Work* (Milton Keynes:
    Open University Press, 1986).
Sherry, Vincent, *The Uncommon Tongue: The Poetry of Geoffrey Hill* (Ann
    Arbor: University of Michigan Press, 1987).
Silkin, Jon, 'The Poetry of Geoffrey Hill', in *British Poetry Since 1960*, edited
    by Michael Schmidt and Grevel Lindop (Manchester: Carcanet, 1972).
Stand, Geoffrey Hill special issue, Vol. 3 No. 4 – Vol. 4 No. 1 (2002).
Walker, Peter, '"The Question of God": Geoffrey Hill's "De Anima"', paper
    given to the colloque, *La Poésie de Geoffrey Hill et la modernité*,
    Université de Caen, May 2003, publication forthcoming.

Index